S0-BBM-290

CROSS TRAINING
MANUAL

Dedication

TO
Wes Neal
who taught me to apply
the Scriptures to athletics and to all of life.

GORDON THIESSEN

Cross Training Publishing
P.O. Box 1541
Grand Island, NE 68802

Cross Training Manual

Library of Congress Cataloging-in-Publication Data

ISBN 1-887002-30-8
Thiessen, Gordon
Gordon Thiessen

Cross Training Manual / Gordon Thiessen
Published by Cross Training Publishing, Grand Island, Nebraska 68803

Distributed in the United States and Canada by Cross Training Publishing

Cover illustrator: Jeff Sharpton
Edited by Gordon Thiessen

CONTENTS

Foreword

It is always very difficult to reconcile one's daily life with a personal faith. Sometimes this is particularly difficult in the world of athletics, where emotions run high and the competitive instinct is so strong. We often see people who are normally exemplary Christians display behavior that is hard to reconcile with what we believe their faith to be. I believe that Gordon Thiessen's book, *The Cross Training Manual,* does an excellent job of explaining how an athlete can use Christian principles that allow him or her to demonstrate in their athletic competition the correct attitude, language, and behavior in regard to their faith.

I also believe that the practice of Christian principles can enable an athlete to maximize his or her potential.

Tom Osborne
Head Football Coach
University of Nebraska

Introduction

Have you ever heard a sermon on playing sports from a biblical perspective? If so, you're one of few. I realize of course, that most church worship settings may not be the best platform for dealing with such a narrowly defined topic. But almost all of us are affected by sports.

You might think that God doesn't have anything to say about athletics. Nothing could be further from the truth. God puts great emphasis on what we say and do. The Bible says in Colossians 3:23 that, "Whatever you do, work at it with all your heart, as working for the Lord, not for men." "Whatever" includes how we train, play and view our sports.

I wrote this book so I can make others aware of God's concern and instruction in living out our lives in the sports arena.

I committed my life to Christ during my freshman year in college. I was on scholarship to play football for the University of Nebraska. My entire life had revolved around athletics, and in particular football. As a Christian, I began to see that God had called me to a different way of life. My behavior needed an overhaul. Before becoming a Christian my language, work habits and perspective on sports were taken from a world that knew little of God's game plan.

Two things happened in my life that changed the way I looked at sports. First, God's Word became a playbook for my training program. To my surprise, I found many passages of Scripture that related to sports.

Secondly, I read the *Handbook on Athletic Perfection*, by Wes Neal. The book related biblical principles to athletics. It became more clear to me what God wanted, and then it was a matter of just doing it.

I had the opportunity to spend three years with Wes Neal's organization, The Institute for Athletic Perfection. The purpose of the organization was to teach athletes to apply God's Word to their athletics. During the three years I had the opportunity to study, discuss and teach many Bible principles from their seminars and materials. I also had a chance during this time to coach the principles I had applied in my own training.

During the past five years I have worked full-time with the Fellowship of Christian Athletes in Central Nebraska. I felt the need to put down on paper some of the things God has taught me in the area of athletics.

I want this book to be a catalyst to change the way you train and play sports. I want God's Word to make a difference in how you live your life. Dr. John MacArthur said, "Only the athlete with the spiritual dimension of Jesus Christ in his life can truly reach his full potential." I believe if you commit your life to Christ, and apply the biblical principles outlined in this book, then you'll have the opportunity to reach your full potential.

How To Use The Cross Training Manual

This manual is designed for athletes who want to become better Christians and athletes. The manual is divided into eight chapters. Each chapter is divided into four sections. The following is a description of how to get the most from each chapter and section.

• **Instruction**
Read and review each chapter. The chapters are designed to teach you how God's Word applies to your athletics.

• **Training Assignment**
This is your chance to apply the biblical principles from each chapter. This section includes Bible memorization, key thought, prayer, and athletic application.

• **Huddle Discussion**
The Huddle Discussion is good for group discussion of the biblical principles covered in the chapter. These questions help you get everyone in your group talking.

• **Wind Sprints**
This section includes several questions to help you dig a little deeper into God's Word to discover more application to your athletics. The questions in this section were developed for personal study.

Along with the eight Huddle Discussions, there is a special section in the Appendix that includes three additional discussion studies for athletes. The *Just Grow for It.* series will challenge you to grow in your faith.

For Use with a Small Group (2-12)

While there are probably many ways to study this book, let me suggest a method that I've found to be helpful.

1) At your first meeting, discuss how you plan to cover the material and what some of your goals are for the group.

2) As a group, discuss the Huddle Discussion section. This will serve as an introduction to the subject to be covered later in the chapter. The *Leading Off* questions are used as ice-

breaker questions. It is not necessary to use them, but you may find them helpful in loosening up the group for discussion.

3) Have the group read chapter one for your next meeting. They should mark or highlight questions or comments from the chapter they find interesting or helpful in the chapter. Assign the Wind Sprints questions for your next meeting.

4) Ask each person in the group to do the Training Assignments. The next time you meet you can discuss any problems or questions they have on this section.

5) Ask the group for any comments or thoughts they have written down or highlighted in the chapter. In your remaining meetings, you'll be able to discuss the Wind Sprints section in each chapter.

For Use with a Large Group (more than 12)

1) Outline the chapter that you plan to cover at your meeting. Present the chapter in a brief talk (10-15 minutes). Whenever possible, use your own illustrations and personal experiences in the talk.

2) Split the group up into smaller groups of four. Then appoint a discussion leader in each group. Make sure each group has a copy of the *Cross Training Manual.* Have each group cover the Huddle Discussion questions. Allow for about 20-25 minutes of discussion.

3) Have each group briefly share their thoughts, comments or conclusions.

Cross Training Workout

The *Cross Training Workout* is described in detail in the Appendix. While the *Cross Training Manual* will coach you on how to grow and compete as a Christian athlete, *Cross Training Workout* will provide you with the necessary spiritual exercises to help you grow in your faith.

You should consider having each member of your group get a copy of the *Cross Training Workout*.It is a simple, yet complete exercise program geared for anyone who wants to grow in their faith. Just as many weightlifters use a workout plan and journal to become stronger, in a similar way the *Cross Training Workout* will help you become stronger in your faith.

Win God's Way

"We win when we do the best we can, where we are, with what we have, to please God."

WINNING

There were many winners and losers in the 1980 Winter Olympic games. The biggest surprise was splashed across the Monday morning sports pages. Most United States newspapers printed headlines like this one by the *Los Angeles Times*. *"THE AMERICAN DREAM TURNS TO GOLD."*

Something incredible happened. A bunch of inexperienced college kids and minor league players (all in their teens and early 20's) beat the best in international hockey—the Soviets who had not lost an Olympic hockey game in 12 years!

Everyone except a coach and few young men said it couldn't be done. Two weeks before it was an unattainable dream. America went wild as their team was able to tie the Swedes, whip the Czechs, beat the Russians and come from behind to win against the Finns 4-2 for the final victory.

An American dream came true. We won and they lost. For everyone who won, victory was sweet. The American hockey players were met with crowds of enthusiastic fans. There was no doubt in our minds that this team represented the pinnacle of success.

What kind of a season did you have last year in your sport? Most likely you judged the success of your season by how many games you won and lost. Very few teams keep records for good sportsmanship. Baseball legend Leo Durocher's famous quote reflects this attitude: "Nice guys finish last!"

There is such a strong emphasis on winning that most of us hate to lose. Most athletes admire a good loser, just as long as it isn't them. We don't mind a winning coach talking about the merits of competition and character building that accompanies losing, but we don't dare let a losing coach get away with it. Sportscaster and former basketball coach, Al McGuire, made the news when he said, "Winning is only important in war and surgery." It's a lot easier to say that when your program is successful. I recently heard of a college coach who was assured that his future with the team was not based on his ability to win games that season. Much to his surprise he was dismissed following the season because his team lost too many games. Baseball manager Tommy LaSorda once said, "Winning isn't everything, but losing is nothing."

What's the point of competition anyway? If all we're supposed to be doing is having fun, why put all the effort and time into our sport? Most would agree that a part of competition is finding out which team performs better on that given day. Vince Lombardi said, "If winning isn't so important, why do they keep score?" Most of us even keep score in pick-up basketball games.

What is Winning & Losing?

The most common definition of winning is to "defeat your opponent." We only need to reverse that definition to find out that losing is to "be defeated by your opponent." It's simple isn't it? All you have to do is glance up at the scoreboard at the end of a game to see who won.

Remember the scene that Kirk Gibson stole out of *The Natural*. His heroic home run that helped the Los Angeles Dodgers win the World Series is embedded in our minds. How about the "Hail Mary" pass by Doug Flutie? We love winning and we agonize in defeat.

How about the losers in the 1980's? Remember Northwestern, Columbia, and Gerry Faust? A lot of people would like to forget them. The winners might feel elated, but check out the losers' lockeroom and it can get nasty. In 1972, the U.S. Olympic Basketball team lost a controversial final game in the last three seconds to the Russians. Not only did America go into mourning over our first defeat in Olympic basketball, but we felt that we had been robbed.

Problems with Winning & Losing

There are at least four problems caused by a winning and losing philosophy based upon the scoreboard.

1. *An overemphasis on winning causes us to have a wrong view of ourselves.* If we're on top there is a tendency for our egos to over inflate, or if we're at the bottom we feel worthless. Neither view is Biblical.

Former tennis star Chris Evert said, "Tennis has been my world since I was six. Tennis molded my personality, defined who I was. Every day I woke up, my moods were subject to tennis: Did I win or lose? I had a high esteem for myself following victory, the opposite after a loss. It's so difficult to cut yourself away from that."[1]

Steve Howe, former Los Angeles Dodger star, had a similar problem with self-esteem, "When I was on the baseball field, that's where I got all my self-esteem, and so my values were placed in wins and losses."[2]

We need to see ourselves as God sees us. "For by the grace given me I say to every one of you: Do not think of yourself more highly than you ought, but rather think of yourself with sober judgment, in accordance with the measure of faith God has given you" (Romans 12:3). God measures our worth by who we *are* as His children, not by how much we accomplish. Our worth should not be based on our accomplishments, credentials, or position on the team.

2. *Overconfidence and lack of concentration caused by focusing on the scoreboard.* You ease up in competition when you are too far ahead. The fear of every coach with a large half-time lead is that his team will lose the intensity it had in the first half of the game. Great comebacks are often caused more by the team in the lead being overconfident than by the efforts of the opposing team.

Overconfidence probably played a role in the USC victory over rival Notre Dame in 1974. It was the biggest game of the year. USC was the defending NCAA football champions and Notre Dame had been their rival since 1926.

The Irish dominated the first half, taking a 24-6 lead. USC's only score in the first half came on a pass from Pat Haden to Anthony Davis with 10 seconds remaining.

In just 16 minutes and 54 seconds, the University of Southern California exploded for 55 points in the second half. Everyone was in shock! It was one of the most lopsided comebacks in college football history. Trojans 55, Irish 24. No doubt many of the Irish players were affected by their total dominance of the first half. It's normal to ease up mentally when you become overconfident. And the Irish had good reason to be confident based upon the scoreboard.

When the Twins star catcher, Brian Harper, was trying to break into the major leagues, God taught him the right perspective on success. "I was struggling and started to think, "What am I going to do if I don't play baseball?", said Brian. "I was 27 and in the minor leagues, and I wasn't doing real well. I had to seek the Lord."

"The Lord impressed upon my heart that there were some things I needed to stop concentrating on and some things I needed to start concentrating on," he said. "I needed to seek Him and seek after the things that He wants me to do rather than seek success in baseball."[3]

His change in perspective made a big difference. He went on to play for the Twins and was voted the most improved player on the team. During the 1990 season his 25-game hitting streak was tops in the majors.

The Christian athlete needs to look beyond the scoreboard. A lack of concentration, caused by focusing on the world's view of success, can be overcome. As you'll see from this chapter there is more to winning than only focusing on the scoreboard.

3. *Nervousness caused by a wrong perspective on winning.* Almost without exception, when a basketball team has the chance to win the game with a last second free throw the opposition will call a time out. They figure if they give the

player shooting the free throw enough time to think about the importance of the shot, he might choke. Undue pressure causes us to tighten up and blow opportunities that might otherwise be routine. If winning is so important that we can't concentrate on doing our job, it has become too important.

In the women's 400 meter relay at the 1936 Olympics, the German team was under great pressure to perform. Adolf Hitler was trying to prove his theory of racial superiority. In the semifinal heat, the Germans had set a new world record. The American team was only .7 seconds slower in their heat. Helen Stephens, of the American team, was the fastest woman in the world, but the German team had a plan to overcome her speed. They planned to lead with their three fastest girls and build up a big lead so that not even Helen Stephens could catch them. The third runner had an 8-meter lead when she passed the baton to Ilse Dorffeldt for the final lap. The German runner became so nervous from the pressure of the world's fastest runner coming from behind and the eyes of Adolf Hitler on her, that she missed the pass of the baton. As a result of the intense pressure she felt, she was unable to concentrate on doing her job and dropped the baton.

Former Seattle Mariner outfielder, Phil Bradley, used to struggle with being anxious about his baseball career. He was impressed by the way several of his teammates, who were Christians, handled winning and losing. Because of their influence he accepted Jesus Christ as his Lord and Savior. As his Christian faith has grown, so has his ability to trust God with his baseball career. "I can relax now," Phil says. "Things don't get to me the way they used to. The thing you constantly have to remind yourself is that Jesus Christ has a plan for you."[4]

4. *Temptation to cheat, which is an outgrowth of an obsession with winning.* If you have any doubts about this, just look at all the problems that college football has had in recent years. The win-at-all-cost pressures have led many schools down the path of cheating. During 1989, twenty-two schools were on NCAA probation, including schools like Houston, Oklahoma State, Oklahoma, Texas A & M and TCU.

If this win-at-all-cost perspective creates problems, what's the alternative? True winning may not be what you think. True winning in the biblical sense has to do with inward character qualities. God's idea of winning is different from man's. As always, God's view of life works best.

How God Measures Winning and Losing

When I entered college at the University of Nebraska, my idea of success or being a winner was to start on the football team and win the mythical National Championship. It was not only important to me, but to the whole state of Nebraska. While I was in college to get an education, football got most of my time and attention. Being a winner to me was starting on a National Championship team.

After committing my life to Jesus Christ, during my freshman year, I started to rethink my view of winning and

losing. I began to think that maybe the world's yardstick of measuring success was wrong. Eventually, I read a booklet called *Total Release Performance,* by Wes Neal. It helped me to see that God had something to say about winning and losing.

As I began to study the Bible, I could see winning and losing are determined by our attitude toward God and men. There is a scoreboard on earth and a scoreboard in heaven, and they're entirely different. We win when we do the best we can, where we are, with what we have, to please God. When we don't do the best we can, we lose. The world views a person as successful if they're the best. God is more concerned with you doing your best and honoring Him.

God's view of winning and losing is not just a matter of keeping statistics. John Wooden, former UCLA basketball coach, believes in a different measure of success than the typical standards, like attaining power or prestige. "Success is not necessarily beating an opponent and scoring more points than they do. If you're good enough, you'll eventually outscore the other team. I didn't want our teams to be better than someone else. I wanted them to be the best they could be."[5]

God wants us to be winners, in the biblical sense. Scripture says that the man who walks in the way of the Lord, "In whatever he does, he prospers" (Psalm 1:3).

Game Plan for Winning

In Joshua, Chapter 1, God gives us a plan for being successful.

"This book of the law shall not depart from your mouth, but you shall meditate on it day and night, so that you may be careful to do according to all that is written in it; for then you will make your way prosperous, and then you will have success." (Joshua 1:8)

God's game plan is to know His Word, meditate on it and obey it. If you learn to be obedient to God's Word, you'll be successful in your athletics. The most important playbook for you to know and apply is God's.

How to WIN!

There are several Bible verses that provide a foundation for real winning. I use the following sentence to remember these principles for winning.

Whatever you do, do your best

to **I**nvest your talents

in the **N**ame of the Lord.

There are three phrases in this sentence that build a biblical foundation for winning from God's perspective.

1. *Whatever you do, do your best...*

"Whatever you do, work at it with all your heart, as working for the Lord, not for men." (Colossians 3:23)

The word "whatever" includes everything you do as an athlete. Whether you play basketball or volleyball, this verse applies to you. It even applies to both practices and games.

The tendency is to slack off during practice, but as you'll see from this verse, that would be wrong.

To "work at it with all your heart" refers to giving it your best shot! It means giving your best mentally, emotionally, and physically in your athletic performance. Christians are to play with intensity! When I think of intensity, I'm reminded of Mike Singletary of the Chicago Bears. You can see the intensity in his eyes, just before the snap of the football. He gives his best effort on every play.

Paul instructs us on the kind of attitude we should have toward our athletics in the book of Romans.

"Work hard and do not be lazy. Serve the
Lord with a heart full of devotion." (Romans 12:11)

I'll never forget how my high school basketball team would try to trick our coach. We would run laps around the gym and splash water on our faces and shirts to look like we had worked hard. We can fool a coach sometimes, but we can never trick God. 1 Samuel 16:7 says, "But the Lord said to Samuel, 'Do not consider his appearance or his height, for I have rejected him. The Lord does not look at the things man looks at. Man looks at the outward appearance, but the Lord looks at the heart.'"

Mike Moore, pitcher for the Oakland A's, sums up this attitude. "I know if I give 100 percent to Christ, then I've done all I can do. If I go out and things happen like they did last night [speaking of a 10-4 loss at Kansas City], I can still hold my head high."[6]

The last part of Colossians 3:23 gives us the key component in defining winning: "working for the Lord, not for

men." Even if we have a give-it-all-you've-got philosophy, we must work to please the Lord, not men, including coaches, parents, teammates, and friends. It doesn't mean we don't care about what others think, but our primary focus is on God, not men. Who do you play for?

Who you play for can help you maintain a proper perspective on your sports. Greg Gagne, Minnesota Twins shortstop, said, "I try to keep baseball in perspective and focus on what Christ says about who I am. And that's that I'm a child of God. I just want to perform for one Person, that's Jesus. I'm doing the best I can for Him, and not trying to please everybody else."[7]

Sports Illustrated questioned whether Christian athletes were as competitive as nonChristian athletes. The notion that Christian athletes don't give as much effort is false, because Christians who play for Jesus Christ have the greatest reason to be intense when they compete. The California Angeles baseball player, Gary Gaetti, said, "Anybody that says I would be docile about losing, I'd challenge him to stand in front of home plate with the ball and try to block me, and see if I have lost my intensity to play."[8] Other athletes were asked the same thing and said, "Just because I'm a Christian doesn't mean I'm a wimp,"[9] said Orel Hershiser of the Dodgers. Tim Burke, baseball reliever for the Mets, said, "If Jesus were on the field, He'd be pitching inside and breaking up double plays. He'd be high-fiving the other guys. That's what Christianity is supposed to be. Some people lose their fire, but not because of the Lord."[10] Tom Landry, former Dallas Cowboy

Coach, argues that faith actually helps an athlete play better. "Faith frees a person to do his best."[11]

2. ... to Invest your talents

The second phrase that builds a biblical foundation for winning from God's perspective involves your talents. Most of us are comfortable with keeping statistics to gauge our success. While we've discussed in this chapter that there are problems with looking to the scoreboard for our definition of true winning. There is another way to look at winning and look at it with a broader perspective. I call this the Success Ratio. It's based on the parable Jesus taught on using our talents in Matthew 25:14-30.

EFFORT: Involves a Christlike attitude/action.
ABILITY/TALENT: Your God given abilities and talents.

If you have the ability of Michael Jordan, you might put down a 10 for ability or talent. If you then give a poor effort during practice, which includes mental, physical and emotional aspects, then you might put down a 5. Your ratio would be 5/10 or a .50. An athlete with lesser talent (5), who gives a great effort (10), would rate 10/5 or a 2. While this formula is very subjective, it should help you look beyond the scoreboard to what real winning involves.

Doing your best with what you have, in a Christlike way, is the key. Mike Gartner, the high scoring NHL hockey

player, said, "As long as I can look myself in the mirror and say I've done my best with the talent the Lord has given me, then I can, without question, say I have been successful. I can only do what I'm capable of doing."[12] Betsy King, one of the top female golfers, shares this view. "My goal is to give 100 percent on every shot. That's the only thing I have control over."[13]

3. *... in the Name of the Lord.* Another verse that relates to God's philosophy of winning is Colossians 3:17, "And whatever you do, whether in word or deed, do it all in the name of the Lord Jesus, giving thanks to God the Father through him." The "whatever you do" includes your athletics and everything else you do in life. Doing it in the name of the Lord is the idea of representing Him by your attitudes and actions.

Sport magazine, when reporting on the recent conversion of baseball star Darryl Strawberry said, "Last winter, Strawberry jumped in to Christianity like Greg Louganis jumps into a pool—head first and deep."[14] The reporter went on to explain that his new found faith was now intertwined with his personality and baseball. That's the way it should be when someone commits their life to Christ. Your faith should intertwine with every area of your life—including athletics.

The film, *Chariots of Fire,* shows the contrast between competing for self or for God. The movie tells the story of two

runners: Harold Abrahams and Eric Liddle. Both ran for Great Britian in the 1924 Olympic Games, but their approach to winning was very different.

Harold Abrahams competed to prove himself to everyone. His desire to win-at-all-cost led him to hire a private coach and train in seclusion to prepare for the Olympic Games.

Abrahams philosophy of winning and losing was based on the scoreboard approach to success. He said, "I don't run to take a beating; if I can't win, I won't run. I run to win." His perspective on winning affected his attitude toward competing. Just before his race in the Olympics, he admitted, "I've known the fear of losing. I'm almost too frightened to win."

Meanwhile, Eric Liddle ran not for his glory, but for God's. He explained his desire to his sister when he said, "God made me fast. When I run, I feel His pleasure. To win is to honor Him." During the Olympic Games, someone said of Eric: "He ran in God's Name, and the world stood back in wonder."

A great example, from the Bible, of someone who understood what it meant to do things in the name of the Lord is David. Everyone is familiar with the story of David and Goliath. Goliath is the highly rated champion of the Philistines team. The game of the week includes a showdown with Goliath, as the undefeated giant, against David the underrated runt from Israel. David didn't have much strength and size, but what he possessed was a faith in the living God. He announced to Goliath that, "You come against me with sword and spear and javelin, but I come against you in the name of the Lord Almighty, the God of the armies of Israel, whom you have defied" (1 Samuel 17:45).

David wasn't concerned with impressing scouts or fans. His only interest was in serving God. He gave everything he had mentally, physically and emotionally to defeat his opponent. He gave his best effort and left the results to God.

The giants we face today may not be nine feet tall, but the principles are still the same. Winning is important, but only if it's the right kind, and only when we pursue it according to God's game plan. We may not finish with more points on the scoreboard, but if we give our best to please God and glorify Him, we become winners each time we compete.

JUST REMEMBER IT.

"Whatever you do, do your work heartily for the Lord, rather than for men." (Colossians 3:23)

JUST THINK IT.

I win when I do my best, where I am, with what I have, to please God.

JUST DO IT.

Write out Colossians 3:23 on a several 3X5 cards. Put the cards on your locker, bathroom mirror, or any other location you pass often. Use the cards as a reminder to give your best effort for God.

JUST PRAY IT.

"Lord, help me to see winning and losing with your eyes. Thank you for the abilities you've given me. Help me make the most of them. Amen."

HUDDLE DISCUSSION

Winning & Losing: God's Way

LEADING OFF: If you could chose any athlete to autograph his or her name for you, who would you chose? Why?

Name an athlete you think of as "successful": Nominate the most successful athlete and vote for the winner.

Babe Ruth, one of the greatest home run hitters of all time, hit sixty home runs in a season, a record that stood for a decade. That same year, however, Ruth set another record—for strike outs. Was he successful? Why or why not?

"God wants all Christian athletes to be winners." (Check one)
❑ True ❑ False Defend your answer.

Which of the following team records do you consider successful? Why?
a. 2-13 b.5-10 c. 7-8 d.8-7
e. 15-0 f. 10-5 g.13-2 h.6-9 i. 9-6

Following a baseball game, the losing pitcher said, "It was God's will that I lost." Do you agree or disagree? Explain.

You will know you are successful in your sport (personally) when you have...

When your athletic career is over, what do you want people to remember about you?

"You're only as good as your last performance." (Check one)
❑ True ❑ False Defend your answer.

Jim wants to win so bad that he often loses his temper on the basketball court. He is a Christian, but has problems applying his faith to his sports. What advice would you give him?

Read the following Scriptures and write out what you think each verse has to say about success: Colossians 3:23 • 2 Corinthians 5:20 • Colossians 3:17 • Acts 5:1-4

WIND SPRINTS

Winning & Losing: God's Way

1. How does Romans 12:3 relate to your attitude? Do you think too much of yourself? Too little? Why?

2. According to Psalm 1:3 how do you think God wants you to prosper? Why?

3. How does Joshua 1:8 apply to your success in athletics?

4. How is Colossians 3:23 more than "just giving it all you've got?"

5. Read Matthew 25:14-30. Using the Success Ratio discussed in this chapter, rate your most recent performance. How could you have improved your ratio?

6. According to 2 Corinthians 5:20 how can you represent Jesus in your sport? If someone evaluated your practices or competitions, how would they know that you are a Christian based on your attitude and effort?

7. What does it mean to set your mind on "the things above" in Colossians 3:2. How does putting your attention on "the things above" affect your athletics?

8. Why are Ananias and Sapphira losers in Acts 5:14? How does this example relate to your sport?

9. What does it mean to "do all in the name of the Lord Jesus" in Colossians 3:17? How can you apply this verse to your athletics?

10. What are some things you should frequently focus on? (Phil. 4:8).

Pursue God's Ultimate Goal

"You are to glorify God in your athletics."

CHAPTER 2

CROSS TRAINING MANUAL

GOAL

Having a goal can push you toward your potential. Gary Smalley gives an example of this in his book, *The Key to Your Child's Heart.*

San Francisco, 1957. A tall, skinny ten-year-old schemed how to sneak inside Kaiser Stadium. All year he had waited for this game between the San Francisco '49ers and the Cleveland Browns. It represented his one chance to see his idol, Jim Brown, the all-pro running back who held almost every rushing record in the NFL.

The boy knew he could slip in when the gate guard left after the third quarter, but even then it wouldn't be easy. Ghetto life had taken its toll on the boy; malnutrition made his legs weak and bowed and he had trouble walking. He needed steel splints just to get around.

Even so he made his way into the stadium and stood right in the middle of the entrance to the players' tunnel. There he patiently waited for the game to end. As the final gun went off, the wiry lad struggled to stand tall so he wouldn't miss his moment. At last he saw Brown turn the corner and walk toward him. The boy held out a piece of paper and politely asked his idol for an autograph. Brown graciously signed it, then turned for the locker room.

> Before he could get away the boy tugged on his jersey and proudly confessed, "Mr. Brown, I have your picture on my wall. My family can't afford a TV set, but I watch you on the neighbor's set every chance I get. I know what your records are and I think you're the greatest. You're my idol."
>
> Brown put his hand on the boy's shoulder and thanked him before heading to the locker room. But the boy reached up and tugged Brown's jersey again. Brown turned and looked into the boy's big brown eyes and asked impatiently, "Yes?"
>
> The boy cleared his throat and said matter-of-factly, "Mr. Brown, one day I'm going to break every one of your records."
>
> "What's your name, son?" he asked.
>
> "Orenthal James, sir, "the boy answered, "but my friends just call me O.J."
>
> In 1973, O.J. Simpson broke Brown's long-standing single-season NFL rushing record and became the first player to gain more than two thousand yards rushing in one year. He was second behind Brown in yardage when injuries forced him to retire.[1]

Having a goal early in life, and pursuing it vigorously helped O.J. Simpson become one of the greatest running backs to play football.

A Goal Defined

A goal is defined as *something toward which you direct your efforts in order to achieve a desired outcome.*

The Importance of Goals

Most coaches would agree that goal setting is a crucial part of success in athletics. "Aim at nothing and you'll probably hit it," someone said referring to the importance of goals. Another quotation often mentioned is, "If you don't know where you're going, you'll probably end up somewhere else." And finally, "If you fail to plan, you plan to fail."

Teams that have a well-developed strategy for their season will often sit down and write out both personal and team goals. What you're aiming at will often help to determine what kind of an athlete or team you will become. If you've set your goal to become first string on the basketball team, it's likely that you'll give your time and effort toward that purpose.

The importance of goals was demonstrated in an experiment by Skip Rose. In Say Yes to *Your Potential*, he describes an experiment done with six basketball teams. Each team was told to shoot one hundred free throws and record their percentage of goals. Two teams were told to spend several hours a day for two weeks practicing to improve their percentage. Two other teams were sent onto a basketball court and told to spend half their time practicing free throws, attempting to make their percentage better. The other half of the time the teams were told to sit and practice free throws in their imaginations.

> The last two teams were told only to practice imagining shooting free throws over and over. But they were helped with how to picture the scene in their mind. Rose suggested the following:
>
> Imagine you are standing at the free throw line. The ball game is over, but you were fouled at the

> buzzer. Your team trails by one point, and you have two free throws. If you make them, your team wins the championship of your league. Feel yourself come to the line, bouncing the ball, calming yourself down. Then feel the release of the ball as you shoot and watch the perfect arch as it swishes through the net. The crowd explodes; the game is tied. You take the ball, you bounce it once, and then you throw it—and it swishes through the net again. The cheers are deafening as the crowd rushes out onto the floor, picks you up and carries you, the hero, away![2]

Following the two weeks of practice the teams were tested again. The first two teams, that had practiced shooting free throws only improved by about one percent. The teams that were told to practice half the time and image half the time also increased by about one percent. But the teams that were told how to visualize the scenario improved 4 1/2 percent. This experiment, along with many other studies, suggests that imagining a goal is nearly as powerful as reality.

Should a Christian Athlete Set Goals?

If Christians are to be content with their circumstances, isn't it wrong to set goals? "Be content with what you have" (Hebrews 13:5). The difficulty in understanding where goals fit into athletics boils down to an understanding of contentment. The following are two possible definitions of Biblical contentment.

✔ I should limit my goals to what I have and what I have already achieved.

✔ I should limit my goals to what I am convinced God wants me to have and to what God wants me to achieve.

The difference between the two definitions is laziness. A proper understanding of contentment involves putting Christ at the center of your life, which includes athletics.

The Apostle Paul uses athletic imagery in 1 Corinthians 9:24-27 to make a point about the Christian life and goals.

Verse 24:...*those who run in a race... Run...that you may win.*
Verse 25:...*Everyone who competes in the games exercises self-control in all things.*
Verse 26:...*I run ...I box...*
Verse 27:...*I buffet my body and make it my slave...*

Paul tells us in these verses that the Christian life is an aggressive pursuit of life, rather than a laid-back attitude. Besides this aggressive life style, Paul points toward the necessity of having a goal.

Verse 24:...*all run, but only one receives the prize. Run in such a way that you may win.*
Verse 26:...*I run in such a way, as not without aim; I box in such a way, as not beating the air.*

The Bible has many examples of men who had goals. Abraham's goal was to follow God anywhere, and gather people around him who would walk by faith. Moses' goal was to rescue the Jews and lead them toward the promised land.

Even the writers of the books of the Bible had goals. When 1 John was written, one of the goals was: "These things have I written to you...that you may know that you have eternal life" (1 John 5:13).

Becoming a good athlete doesn't just happen. You become a better athlete because you set goals, make plans, and take action.

Problems with Goals

It's difficult to choose goals that will glorify God. What do you desire from your athletics? Is it popularity? Money? Trophies? Championships? You can become so wrapped up in your own goals that you can often overlook God's ultimate goal for you.

Goal-Setting

Where are you going? How do plan to get there? Setting proper goals is important. You should set goals in every area of your life. You should not only consider athletic goals, but also spiritual, educational, family, and career goals. Your goals can fit into three categories: long-range, short-range and immediate goals. Anything over a year is long-range. Anything under a month is immediate. Anything between a month and one year is short-range.

When setting goals, use the acronym **S-A-M**. When you set your goals make sure they are Specific, Achievable, and Measurable.

S—Specific

Most athletes set goals that are too general. You should be very specific about your goals. Make sure they can be achieved during a set time period.

Wrong: "I'm going to start lifting weights this season." Too general; It may never happen, since it's only a good idea. Right: "I'm going to bench press three days a week and do at least six sets."

Wrong: "I'm going to improve my serving in volleyball." Too general; How will you improve it?
Right: "I'm going to work 15 minutes each day on improving my serve by watching videos on successful serves."

A—Achievable

A lot of goals are unrealistic. In fact, some are impossible! I knew one athlete that planned to grow from 5'10" to 6' by his senior year! There is no way he could control or affect how much he would grow. It was a totally unrealistic goal.

"I'm going to lead the NBA in points." Unless you're Michael Jordan, you better rethink this goal. It's not always easy to set a goal that will stretch you, yet is realistic.

It's important to set goals high enough so that you are stretched by them. Reggie White of the Philadelphia Eagles, perhaps the best defensive player in pro football, said, "If you're set on being mediocre, you'll reach your goal. I'm committed to excellence."[2]

Your goals should be difficult, but achievable. If you've ever lifted weights, you understand the value of setting your goal just beyond what you can do. To increase your strength, you lift weights that are difficult but realistic enough to build your muscles.

M—Measurable

You should set your goals so you can tell when you reach them. It's important to evaluate yourself before you set your goals.

"I'm going to spend more time running sprints." What does "more time" mean? It's better to say, "I'm going to run three 200 meter sprints under 25 seconds after each practice." Now you know how many and when you're going to run the sprints.

Evaluation Questions

The following are several questions, which will help make you more sensitive to what goals God would have you pursue.

1. Will my goals glorify God or are they selfish?
"So ... whatever you do, do all for the glory of God" (1 Corinthians 10:31).

2. Did I pray about my goals?
"This is the confidence we have in approaching God: that if we ask anything according to his will, he hears us" (1 John 5:14).

3. How will my goals affect others?
"... Therefore if what I eat causes my brother to fall into sin, I will never eat meat again, so that I will not cause him to fall" (1 Corinthians 8:11-13).

4. How will my goals affect me?
"Everything is permissible"—but not everything is beneficial." (1 Corinthinans 10:23).

5. What would Jesus do?
"And whatever you do, whether in word or deed, do it all in the name of the Lord Jesus, giving thanks to God the Father through him" (Colossians 3:1). Mike Moore, Oakland Athletics pitcher, said, "When I go out, I'm not just trying to compete for myself. A lot of times I think what He [God] would do in this situation. I wouldn't think He'd be afraid to knock somebody off the plate."[3]

You may not have as much talent as a Mike Moore, but God can still take whatever talent you have to serve Him with your life. Tanya Crevier, the "World's Finest Female

Basketball Handler", let God use her talents, regardless of her being small and slow. She often tells others that, "God can use any of our talents—He gave them to us in the first place. The most important thing was that I loved God and somehow wanted to use my talents for Him. God can use any talent we have as long as we're faithful to Him, as long as we set proper goals mentally, physically, and spiritually. God will keep expanding our opportunities as we keep turning things over in our life to Him and allow Him to guide and direct us."[4]

God's Ultimate Goal

While you may set-up goals in many areas of your life, there is only one ultimate goal. You are to glorify God in your athletics. You do this by being Christlike. Archie Griffin, the only player to be awarded the Heisman Trophy twice, set several goals. While he was exceeding his expectations on the gridiron, he was also hitting the books in the classroom. Those were not his only goals. He maintains that his primary ambition—since asking Jesus Christ to be his Savior at the age of 13—has been to serve Him. This idea helped him keep the right perspective of himself and his career. "I believe the ability I have is from God."[5]

If you do things God's way, it doesn't necessarily guarantee that you'll win every time you take the field. In almost every situation, though, doing things His way will allow you to perform to the best of your abilities.

Goal-setting is important, especially since it can help motivate you to action, but God is more concerned with what you will become than what

you have done. It's possible to do many things in athletics, but be zilch as a person. You can receive all kinds of trophies and prestige, but being Christlike is far more valuable and lasting. Mike Moore, professional baseball pitcher, said, "I want all my actions to be Christlike."[6]

Twice in Colossians 3 we read, "Whatsoever you do...whatever you do..." (vv. 17, 23). It's as if the Lord is saying, "Makes no difference what it is, whatever you do..." But then the Apostle Paul mentions things that relate to being. Like being thankful, being considerate, being obedient, being sincere. God emphasizes being more than He emphasizes doing.

There are several verses that provide the foundation for the Christian athletes' ultimate goal.

"Or do you not know that your body is a temple of the Holy Spirit who is in you, whom you have from God, and that you are not your own? For you have been bought with a price; therefore glorify God in your body."
(1 Corinthians 6:19-20)

This verse need to be applied to your athletics:

I AM NOT MY OWN.
I AM TO GLORIFY GOD.

Your ultimate goal, your greatest mission in athletics is to glorify God. Setting goals to win championships, set records and win games are fine, but glorifying Him should be your greatest pursuit. The writers of the Westminster Shorter Catechism understood this. That's why they wrote: "The chief end of man is to glorify God and to enjoy Him forever."

The word "glorify" can mean to cause somebody to respect and have a good opinion of somebody else. When an athlete is recognized for their outstanding achievements, they are often introduced with a highlight film of their past performances. In a spiritual sense, we become God's highlight film for the world to view, as we glorify him by our actions. As we cause others to respect and have a good opinion of Him—we bring glory to Him, rather than ourselves.

It's possible for a Christian athlete to receive fame and riches, but all that should be secondary. Michael Chang demonstrated this attitude in the spring of 1989 when he stunned the tennis world by becoming the youngest player ever to win the French Open. His endorsements alone exceed one million dollars annually. He looks forward to career winnings that will run into many millions more. But Chang, who makes plain his faith in Christ in television interviews, realizes that all his money and fame are not what his life is all about.

"For me", said Chang, "I feel as if being a Christian, I have a job to do on this earth, and that's my first priority—to get that job done. You can't win all the time. You can only do as much as you are made to do."[7]

Another verse that relates to your ultimate goal of glorifying God is taught by Paul in Romans:

"For whom he foreknew, he also predestined to become conformed to the image of his Son, that he might be the first born among many brethren..." (Romans 8:29)

Not only did God choose you to spend eternity with Him, but He is also conforming you to the image and likeness of Jesus Christ. He wants you to be changed in every area of your life—thought, actions, character, and attitude. This is an inner process of development that is a lifelong process which brings glory to God.

The process of becoming Christlike is only possible once you have committed your life to Him, but it takes time for you to become like Him. For example,the athlete who struggled with profanity before becoming a Christian might continue to find this area difficult to control. But with time and God's help they can begin to become more like Christ.

The last verse that relates to God's ultimate goal for you is:

"We are therefore Christ's ambassadors, as though God were making his appeal through us." (2 Corinthians 5:20)

An ambassador is someone who acts as a representative for another. It involves being a personal representative. The Apostle Paul teaches us in this passage that God has given us the responsibility to act for Him. We are to be His personal representatives here on earth.

If you want to represent Christ in the athletic arena, then you need to know what He would say and do. As a Christian athlete you have the responsibility to compete in a way that pleases God, and represent Him through your actions.

Glenn Davis, who played with the Houston Astros takes this role seriously. The Astros' television announcers greet every Houston home run with a plug for Budweiser beer, which is a sponsor of the broadcasts. "Glenn Davis (or whoever else hit the homer), this Bud's for you!" they proclaim. Davis asked not to be toasted over the air. "I realize I'm a lone wolf on this," says Davis, "but somebody's got to take the responsibility of providing role models for kids. Athletes are in a position where we can do it."[8]

"Once you're not in the game anymore, people won't remember your stats," he continues. "When I die, I don't want someone to put on my tombstone that I was good in baseball. I want it to say that I had an impact on someone's life."[9] Davis is acting as a representative for God as he believes God would have him act.

The Perfect Role Model

By studying God's Word you can begin to understand how Jesus might react to some of the situations you encounter. Jesus gives you the perfect model to follow. No one else, not even your favorite sports star, is ultimately worthy of being imitated. Paul, in Ephesians 5:1, tells you to imitate God instead: "Be imitators of God." No other model is sufficient, no other deserves your emulation in life. That doesn't mean that would-be basketball greats shouldn't try to fly through the air like Michael Jordan or aspiring quarterbacks shouldn't try to throw like John Elway, but it means that you are to emulate the way Jesus would respond to different situations in sports.

There is no question that athletes are role models for many young people. The image seems to have been tarnished in recent years, but athletes are still the most respected. That's what a poll conducted in 1989 by the Travelers Company showed. When asked what group of professionals is most likely to provide a positive role model for youth, athletes were selected by 37 percent of those polled. Business executives got half as many votes, pop artists 14 percent, politicians and TV/movie stars, 11 percent.

The sports world is full of examples of men and women who appear to be perfect, but the closer you get to them the more ordinary you will find them. They struggle with the same sins that everyone does: selfish ambition, pride, jealousy.

While you need to keep your eyes focused on Jesus as your role model, you must realize that it's only natural that others will look to you as a role model. You need to be careful to point to Jesus as the ultimate role model. Paul told others to follow him, only as he followed Christ.

There is no doubt that God wants His best for you. He is not only interested in your athletics, but the rest of your life as well. Choose goals that will support your ultimate goal, to glorify God. With a little inspiration and perspiration, you'll begin to see your goals accomplished. What is it that you really want of your sport? Go ahead put it to the test and plan for it. The ultimate goal, to glorify God, will help you be all you can be.

JUST REMEMBER IT.

"So ... whatever you do, do all for the glory of God" (1 Cor. 10:31).

JUST THINK IT.

I commit myself to glorifying God in athletics.

JUST DO IT.

Review your goals before each workout.

JUST PRAY IT.

"Lord, Help me to glorify You through my thoughts and actions. Thank you for giving me the opportunity to represent you on the athletic field. Amen."

HUDDLE DISCUSSION

Goal: Pursue God's Ultimate Goal

LEADING OFF: If you could have attended any game in sports history, which one would you choose? Why?

"Sports is a wonderful tool, but a horrible God." In what ways is this statement true?

Describe a goal? Christians should never set goals? True or false? Why or why not? How do you decide if a particular goal is good or bad?

Make a wish list of "goals" you would like to reach during the next year. What goals did you write down? Why did you choose each one? What will it take to reach your goals?

Jill is disappointed in herself for not making the All-City basketball team. She is also upset because her other goal of getting an athletic scholarship will probably not happen. What is her problem? What advice can you give her?

Which of the following questions do you find most helpful when setting goals and why?

- Will my goals glorify God or are they selfish?
- Do I pray about my goals?
- How will my goals affect me?
- What would Jesus do?

Read each of the Bible verses below and complete the sentences using what you learned from the Bible passage. Share your completed sentences with the group.

Romans 8:29
My ultimate goal as a Christian athlete is to...
Colossians 3:23
In whatever game I play I should always...
2 Corinthians 5:20
I have a responsibility to...

WIND SPRINTS

Goal: Pursue God's Ultimate Goal

1. What is a goal?

2. What is the goal Paul mentions in Philippians 3:14? How can it be reached?

3. How should you respond to an opponent who uses intimidation or cheats against you in athletic competition? (See Romans 12:17-21).

4. How does Matthew 6:24 relate to your ultimate goal?

5. What was the goal and prize at which Paul was aiming? (See Phil. 3:14; 2 Timothy 4:6-8).

6. How does Romans 8:29 relate to your athletics?

7. Read 1 Peter 2:21. How can you apply this verse to your athletics?

8. How can you be an ambassador for Christ in your sport? (See 2 Cor. 5:20).

9. Set goals in your athletics, spiritual life, school, family, work, etc.

10. Use the following questions and the SAM acronym to help you set proper goals.

    - Will my goals glorify God or are they selfish?
    - Do I pray about my goals?
    - How will my goals affect me?
    - What would Jesus do?

Give All You've Got for God

"Give your best effort to show your appreciation and respect to God."

CHAPTER 3

MOTIVATION

How important is motivation? Almost all athletes are motivated by something. Our degree of motivation can move us to greatness or leave us wallowing in mediocrity. The following story shows the important role that motivation plays in sports.

A baby named Wilma was born prematurely. Because of this, she contracted double pneumonia and scarlet fever. She had polio, which left her with a crooked left leg and a foot twisted inward. Her legs were placed in metal braces, and Wilma spent six years riding a bus to Nashville, Tennessee for treatments.

Wilma was determined not to let her disability hold her back. She kept working to overcome her handicap and by age eleven forced herself to learn to walk without her braces.

Her determination could be seen in her confrontation with her coach at age twelve. She had a dream and was highly motivated to attain it. She told her coach, "If you will give me ten minutes of your time every day—and only ten minutes—I'll give you a world-class athlete."

Fortunately, he took her up on the offer. Wilma not only won a starting job on the basketball squad, she later decided to try track.

She first beat her girlfriend. Then she went on to beat every girl in her school and then every girl in Tennessee. At only fourteen years of age she was one of the best in the country.

Wilma went on to run in the 1956 Olympic games at Melbourne. She won a bronze medal in the 400-meter relay. A bronze was not enough as she began to train for the next Olympics. Her training program included; running at six and ten every morning and three every afternoon. Wilma would even sneak down the dormitory fire escape from eight to ten o'clock at night and run on the track before bedtime.

Her grueling training schedule paid off. She went on to victory in both the 100-meter and 200-meter dashes. She also anchored the U.S. women's team to a first-place finish in the 400-meter relay. Wilma was the first woman in Olympic history to win three gold medals in track-and-field.[1]

Wilma Rudolph started out life crippled and with little hope to walk. Through hard work and a strong desire to improve, she became one of the best female runners in history. No doubt, motivation played a big part in Wilma becoming a world-class runner.

What separates athletes is not so much their inborn abilities as their motivation. Few athletes live up to their potential. Coaches point out that the difference between the star and the superstar is usually not talent, but motivation. One is willing to pay a price that the other isn't because of motivation.

What is Motivation?

Motivation is important to every athlete or coach. What is it that motivates one athlete to do better than another? What is the motivation to endure physical pain? What is the motivation to keep on going when others are dropping out? Motivation is a powerful factor in athletics, and you need to know what it is and how to apply it.

The Webster Dictionary gives insight into motivation.

Motive

1. That within the individual, rather than without, which incites him to motion; any idea, need, emotion, or organic state that prompts to an action.

Motivate

To provide with a motive; to impel; incite.

Motivation is in your mind. Action is the result of your motivation. You become what you think. Long before coaches used this definition of motivation, the Bible included it in one of its ancient scrolls, "For as he thinks within himself, so he is" (Proverbs 23:7). What you think about during competition is crucial to your athletic performances. Your attitude will reveal itself in your actions.

Kinds of Motivation

All athletes have psychological needs that they would like to fulfill. They have a need for a sense of accomplishment. For example, the sense of accomplishment is important to building self-esteem. They want to feel good about themselves. Whether it is a sixth grader or an NBA star shooting free throws they feel good about themselves when they reach their goals.

There are many different types of psychological needs that athletes have, both good and bad. A coach can appeal to many of them to motivate an athlete. What approach is best? The best approach to take to motivate someone is debatable and varies with the person and the situation.

To motivate an athlete a coach might use fear. Fear of losing a starting position or being yelled at can work. Who hasn't given just a little extra effort to avoid being embarrassed by a coach? This may work for awhile, but as time goes on, many athletes need something else.

Hope of reward is the most common motivation. It might be recognition or monetary reward, or both.

Harvey Dorfman, the Oakland A's psychologist, commented on this need when Rickey Henderson expressed his discontent over a baseball contract. "What Rickey can see clearly is that he has gone from being the second $3 million man to being the 40th," says Dorfman. "And if that is the way society is going to judge him, he wants to ensure that that judgement is corrected. It is not a money issue. His need is for recognition."[2]

Who doesn't enjoy seeing himself in print? Almost every community has at least one trophy shop that caters to the need for recognition that each of us has. Rewards are also dependent upon circumstances. It's fine when we win the gold medal, but what happens when there is little chance for us to win the medal we want? Each year teams that find themselves with no possibility to make the play-offs struggle with motivating their players to perform.

Fame or recognition never lasts.

Ask Muhammed Ali.

You know Ali, the unprecedented three-time world heavyweight boxing champion. His face has appeared on the cover of *Sports Illustrated* more times than any other athlete. When he was "floating like a butterfly and stinging like a bee," he was king of his profession. An entourage of reporters, trainers, and support staff tailed this comet as he raced around the world.

But that was yesterday. Where is Muhammed Ali today? Sportswriter Gary Smith went to find out.

> Ali escorted Smith to a barn next to his farmhouse. On the floor, leaning against the walls were momentos of Ali in his prime. Photos and portraits of the champ punching and dancing. Sculpted body. Fist punching air. Championship belt held high in triumph. "The Thrilla in Manilla."
>
> But on the pictures were white streaks—bird droppings. Ali looked into the rafters at the pigeons who had made his gym their home. And then he did something significant. Perhaps it was a

> gesture of closure. Maybe it was a statement of despair. Whatever the reason, he walked over to the row of pictures and turned them, one by one, toward the wall. He then walked to the door, stared at the countryside, and mumbled something so low that Smith had to ask him to repeat it. Ali did. "I had the world," he said, "and it wasn't nothin'. Look now."[3]

Money can motivate professional athletes to play better to receive a more substantial contract, but often their performance level drops off once they've negotiated that contract. When thinking of the temporary motivation of fame and fortune, I'm reminded of Horace Greely's comment, "Fame is a vapor; popularity an accident. Riches take wing; those who cheer today will curse tomorrow."

Some coaches use revenge or anger to motivate their athletes. Neither is biblical or healthy. Revenge and anger might work temporarily, but it is hard to imagine them working consistently over a period of time.

Just as Mr. Webster was saying in the definition of motives, real motivation comes from within. Athletes motivated from within surpass any achievements they would otherwise have accomplished. All other motivations, the pep-talk, the excitement of the crowd, are external and temporary. They just won't last. They are artificial forms of motivation. Former basketball coach, John Wooden, said, "I never wanted to create an emotional peak for our teams, because for every artificial peak you create, there's a valley."[4]

These kinds of motivation are not always wrong, but the motivation that comes from within is the best. It is more consistent and more powerful. How can an athlete be motivated from within?

Biblical Motivation

The secret to real motivation is in the Bible. God provides us with the greatest motivation in the world. The Apostle Paul gives us insight into Christian motivation in 1 Corinthians 15 where he talks about the grace of God three times in verse 10. "By the grace of God I am what I am." Then he adds that God's grace was not without effect. "I worked harder than all of them." And finally, he says that it was "not I, but the grace of God that was with me."

Paul is motivated by the grace of God. Grace is the root from which gratitude grows. The powerful Christian motivation Paul talks about is to understand the grace of God. Once you understand God's grace, it will give you a tremendous sense of gratitude. If you understand that you are what you are by the grace of God, then you will be consistently motivated to serve God by doing your best.

A great example of someone motivated by God's grace is Chicago Bears linebacker, Mike Singletary. "Many people have asked me about my intensity in the game of football. My intensity as an athlete, husband, and father basically boils down to this: God's grace toward me. It's only grace that allows someone like me to worship the Lord, in return for what He has done for me."[5]

To understand grace we need to take a moment to see how God chose to deal with mankind. God deals with us by mixing justice with mercy and grace. **Justice** gives us what we deserve; **mercy** doesn't give us all we deserve; **grace** gives us what we don't deserve.

Romans 3:23 tells us that, "the wages of sin is death. "If we're to receive what we deserve, then we need to recognize that death is the payment for sin. God had a plan where he could justly give us what we deserve, but mercifully, give it to us in such a way that it wouldn't destroy us. God provided Jesus as a substitute for us. Paul says, "God demonstrates his own love for us in this: While we were still sinners, Christ died for us" (Romans 5:8).

We have the opportunity to live for His glory and be in eternity. It's all because of grace. He made us children of God. He promised us eternal life.

When we experience love, we normally respond by trying to express our love in return. When we think about what God did for us through Jesus taking our place on the cross, it should make us want to show our gratitude toward Him in some way.

As an athlete you can express your gratitude and respect to Jesus! You can be motivated to work harder, achieve more, because you want to please Jesus by your efforts.

God has provided us with a way to show our gratitude toward Him. Paul outlines it in Romans 12:1.

"Therefore, I urge you, brothers, in view of God's mercy, to offer your bodies as living sacrifices, holy and pleasing to God—this is your spiritual act of worship."

When you see the word "therefore", you need to ask, "What's it there for? Paul is referring back to what he has already written about in the book of Romans. He means,

"Because of all the things you have received from God, here is what you need to do." Paul was urgently asking them to make a proper response to all God meant to them.

The reason he was urgently pleading with them was because of God's mercy. God showed His mercy to us through Jesus Christ.

Therefore—and this is the right response—we must offer our bodies "as living sacrifices, holy and pleasing to God." Paul urges us to put ourselves on the altar, like Isaac, who was considered a living sacrifice in the Old Testament. Our bodies, which include our talents and abilities, are to be presented for his service. Just as the sacrificial animals of the Old Testament were to be without spot or blemish, so our lives are to be "holy, acceptable to the Lord." The bottom line is that we are to offer our lives in obedience to God.

It's important to understand what Paul means by "spiritual act of worship." Worship literally means "worth-ship." It's giving worthiness to an individual. It means to pay reverence or to honor. The New Testament uses three different words for worship. The word used most often refers to recognition of the worth of the person. The other two words refer to the attitude one should have and the action one should take as a result of honoring that person. If you put

together the three different thoughts, it involves recognizing worth, granting respect and giving service.

Worship produces service that is glorifying to God. You can serve God through your athletics as an act of worship. You give service to God by your actions which demonstrate your respect for God. Paul teaches that the motivation to serve God makes sense because of His supremacy and mercy. Therefore, it's only logical to give all you have to serve God. Paul argues that we should willfully reserve the totality of our lives for the Lord's good purposes. We're to put ourselves at God's disposal, which includes our athletics.

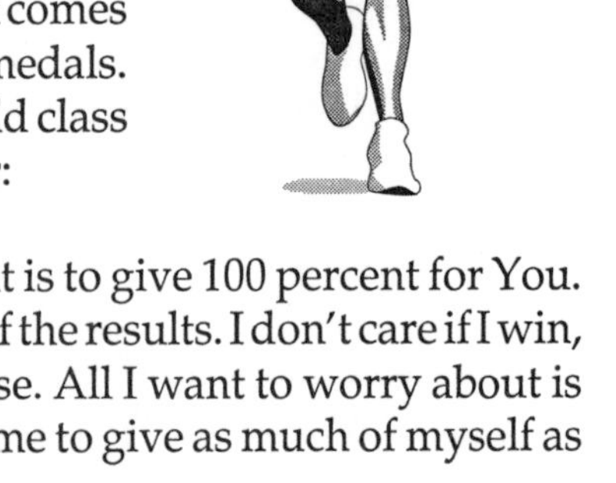

Dave Johnson, the highly ranked decathlete, is motivated by God's grace to give his best efforts to serve God. For Johnson, motivation comes from more than awards and medals. Even before he became a world class athlete he prayed this prayer:

"Lord, here I am. All I want is to give 100 percent for You. I'm trusting You to take care of the results. I don't care if I win, get personal best marks or lose. All I want to worry about is doing my best for You. Help me to give as much of myself as I can."[6]

Jan Ripple, one of the best female triathletes, uses this motivational strategy during her final mile of a race. "When reporters ask me why I compete and put my body through such things, I can honestly say it's because I realize Jesus carried me. He carried the Cross and the persecution and the shame for me. He went through that. This is my last mile and it's not nearly as bad as what He did to carry that Cross."[7]

In the 1924 Olympics, two Englishmen won gold medals. Their story was told in the powerful movie, *Chariots of Fire*. What they achieved was very similar, but their motivation for running were very different. Harold Abrahams ran to gain respect from an establishment that was hostile to Jews. Eric Liddel ran as a Christian. He was motivated to win because of his desire to please his Lord who had given him his talents.

The movie tells the story of Eric's Olympic team taking a trip across the English Channel to compete in the 1924 Games in Paris. During the trip Eric learns that his preliminary heats would be run on Sunday. This was a problem for him since competing on the Lord's day was unacceptable, even if it meant forfeiting the race. The point here is not Sabbath lawbreaking, but his commitment to spiritual values. Eric was pressured by everyone to run in the race, but his motivation to run was not based on acceptance by man. He ran to glorify the Lord.

For Liddel, this was a pattern for his entire life. He later served as a missionary to China, and finally laid down his life while serving others in a Japanese prisoner-of-war camp during World War II.

The greatest example of someone motivated to serve God, was Jesus Christ. His motivation led Him to make the ultimate sacrifice for mankind. His sacrifice was complete—physically, emotionally and spiritually. Here is a brief look at His sacrifice.

Physical

First Jesus sweat blood while He was praying in the Garden of Gethsemane. This is a medically proven condition that can happen when someone endures great emotional stress.

Then a crown of thorns was jammed down on His head. The crown was probably made out of needle-sharp thorns that were between one and two inches long.

Then He was flogged. The Roman soldiers used a whip, which was made of several strips of leather, each one with sharp rocks and pieces of metal attached to it. During the flogging, His back would have been cut open, possibly exposing even the internal organs. He was also beaten by the soldiers beyond recognition.

Then he was crucified. Considered the most painful way to be put to death, they drove heavy spikes through His wrists and feet. He was then raised up on the cross, and it was slammed down into place, probably dislocating His shoulders. Finally, His side was pierced with a sword so that blood and water spilled out.

Emotional

Imagine the emotional pain He felt being striped naked and hung up on a cross for all to see. It must have been difficult to watch his friends and family observe Him being mocked and tortured. He had been let down by his closest friends and was now being rejected by those He came to save.

Spiritual

Jesus was a perfect man who suddenly had to bear the sins of the world. For the first time He was spiritually separated from the Father. He was so close to God that they were actually one. In anguish, Jesus cried out on the cross, "My God, my God why have you forsaken me?" (Matthew 27:46).

Jesus was totally motivated to pay the awesome penalty for sin by dying a gruesome death, and He died after suffering on the cross for six long hours. This was His "spiritual service of worship." It was His way to express His love and respect to His Father by carrying out His Father's plan.

Whom do you play for?

Whom you play for can affect your motivation. A powerful example of this was displayed when the Kansas City Chiefs played the Seattle Seahawks on November 11, 1990.

Linebacker Derrick Thomas sacked quarterback Dave Krieg nine times that day, once on each of the Seahawks' first two possessions, and four times in the decisive fourth period. One of his sacks forced a fumble that was recovered for the Chiefs' only touchdown in three weeks. "That kind of effort is the thing you build championships on," said Chiefs' Coach Marty Schottenheimer.

Just before the game started, four jets flew over the stadium as a tribute to Derrick's father who was an Air Force captain lost in the Vietnam war. The tribute helped inspire Thomas to play for his father. He said, "I guess my father is watching and that inspired me to play my best today."

No doubt Derrick's love and appreciation for his father motivated him to play his best. In a very real sense, God is watching each of us. Can we play with any less intensity than Thomas played for his earthly father? Each time you compete you have the opportunity to show your Heavenly Father that you love and appreciate Him by your actions.

A New Motivation

God's motivation works because it starts from within and is always available. The "gratitude attitude" is logical because it doesn't depend on outside circumstances that wear off.

Since God's motivation is permanent it can make a difference in your athletics. Most athletes would like to make a difference. But you can't make a difference, until you **are** different. The difference is only possible by becoming the new creation that Paul talked about in 2 Corinthians 5:17.

Once you've become that new creation in Christ, you're capable of being motivated by grace to pursue excellence in every area of your athletics! Dwight L. Moody, the great evangelist, was motivated by the words of Charles Spurgeon: "The world has yet to see what God can do with one life totally yielded to Jesus Christ." Moody said to himself, "By the grace of God I'll be that man." Are you ready to be that man or woman and yield your athletics to Him?

JUST REMEMBER IT.
"For as a man thinks within himself, so he is" (Proverbs 23:7).

JUST THINK IT.
I will give my best effort to show my appreciation and respect to God.

JUST DO IT.
During the week, briefly review what Jesus did for you on the cross. Then picture Jesus as your only audience when you compete.

JUST PRAY IT.
"Lord, thank you for sending your Son to die for me. I love you Lord and appreciate what you did in sending Jesus to die on the cross for my sins. I offer myself as a living sacrifice. Amen."

HUDDLE DISCUSSION

Motivation: Give All You've Got for God

LEADING OFF: Who were your sports heroes when you were younger? Now? Why?

In what game did you give your best effort? Why?

Circle the word that best describes what motivates you to give your best effort.

Revenge Anger Recognition Fear Other (explain)
Share your responses with the group and explain.

On your team, how many of your teammates do you think are playing up to their potential? (circle one)
Explain your response.

10% 20% 30% 40% 50% 60% 70%
80% 90% 100%

Which athlete today is the greatest example of someone who gives his or her best effort every competition?

If Jesus Christ were physically present for your practice sessions, would it make a difference in the way you practiced? Why or why not?

The *N.Y. Times* reported that a number of Christian athletes including: Orel Hershiser, Howard Johnson, Kevin Maas, Gary Carter, Tim Burke, Reggie White, Darryl Strawberry, Barry Sanders and Scott Simpson give 10 percent of their income to God. Darryl Strawberry may eventually give $2 million to his church. What do you think motivates these athletes to give? What can you give God, other than money?

Read the following scriptures to discover the perfect motivational force. Discuss how each verse applies to athletics.

John 3:16 • John 13: 34-35 • 2 Samuel 23:13-17

WIND SPRINTS

Motivation: Give All You've Got for God

1. How does the grace of God motivate you?
(See 1 Cor. 15:10).

2. How can Romans 12:1 become a reality in your athletics?

3. How does knowing what Jesus went through on the cross affect your motivation?

4. What does the Bible say about motivation?
(See Proverbs 23:7).

5. How can you express your love and appreciation to God according to Romans 12:1?

6. How does Mark 12:30 relate to your motivation as an athlete?

7. Read 2 Samuel 23:13-17. How did love motivate David's men?

8. Read John 14:15-16. How do these verses relate to motivation?

9. Read 1 Cor. 6:20. How can you apply this verse to your athletics?

10. What were Ananias and Sapphira motivated by in Acts 5:14? What was the result?

Turn Setbacks Into Comebacks

"God is chiseling out your character through the problems and setbacks you face in athletics."

CHAPTER 4

CROSS TRAINING MANUAL

SETBACKS

After he won his first Tour de France in 1986, Greg LeMond, had everything going for him. Fame, fortune and a bright future seemed assured. On April 27, 1987, while turkey hunting, he was accidentally shot. The blast put holes in his back, legs, arms and hands, and he also broke two ribs.

It was the greatest athletic setback Greg LeMond had faced. Rumors began to spread that his sponsors had spent too much for damaged goods. "The last two years have been the most humiliating of my life," reflected LeMond. "Riders and team managers thought I was through, and that made me more determined than ever to return."[1]

His return was nothing short of miraculous! LeMond did what everyone thought was impossible. He overcame a fifty-second deficit in the final stage of the 1989 Tour de France to win by eight seconds. It was one of the most exciting finishes in sports history. It was also the narrowest margin of victory in the history of the race.

Setbacks can make you better or bitter. A lot depends on your perspective. Maybe you've heard the saying, "When life hands you a lemon, make lemonade!" This basic philosophy is both sound and biblical. Many people in the Bible turn defeat into victory and trial into triumph. Almost every athlete, sooner or later, runs headlong into an athletic setback and must choose to be either victim or victor.

Scouting Report on Athletic Setbacks

It's important to understand the impact that setbacks have on athletics. There are at least three common setbacks in athletics.

Emotional setbacks are perhaps the most common. Anytime you lose a game, blow an assignment, or fail to make the team there is an emotional letdown.

On June 4, 1986, Kathy Ormsby, was overcome by her emotions during the NCAA's 10,000-meter race. Before competing in the NCAA Outdoor Championships in Indianapolis, she held the record for the 10,000 meters race. Ormsby was also on the dean's list and was a pre-med major.

During the race she left the track, ran out of the stadium, scaled a 7-foot chain link fence, and jumped off a bridge over the White River. She was critically injured from the fall. "All of a sudden ... I just felt like something snapped inside of me," she said. "And I was really angry. I felt like it was so unfair." The emotional pressures of competition were too much for her.

Nothing is more discouraging to an athlete than a nagging injury. Physical setbacks or injuries become more common each season. As athletes get bigger and faster, the physical risks increase. Joe Theismann's NFL career came to a sudden end during a football game in 1985 when he was sacked by Lawrence Taylor of the New York Giants. Theismann's leg almost snapped in half.

Dave Dravecky, who retired from the San Francisco Giants in 1989, understands the impact physical injuries have on athletes. He had overcome cancer surgery on his throwing arm and had come back to play. Doctors removed the tumor and nearly half of the deltoid muscle on his pitching arm.

On August 10, 1989, a capacity crowd came to see Dravecky make his exciting comeback appearance at home against the Cincinnati Reds. His comeback didn't last. A few games later, at Montreal, the humerus bone in his pitching arm snapped as he delivered a pitch. He fell to the ground in pain, with a broken arm. The setback ended a career that lasted seven years in the majors.

Unfairness is another setback. Almost every day in the sports pages we read that athletes often find themselves in unfair circumstances. Outside forces can affect the outcome of competition. It's easy to see outside forces as unfair.

During the 1984 Olympic Games, Zola Budd and Mary Decker collided in the women's 3000-meter run. Decker fell

to the ground in pain as her dream of Olympic gold was shattered. Neither runner was able to finish the race, and nothing could have seemed more unfair to either athlete. All athletes have to overcome some kind of unfairness in their competition.

Purpose of Setbacks

Why me? When you sprain an ankle, miss an assignment, lose a game or move down in the depth charts you ask this question. It's not always possible to explain or understand setbacks.

God doesn't always give direct answers to the question, "Why?" Sometimes He only shows us the "why" many years later. Clint Hurdle, former major league baseball player, when faced with the fact that he would not reach many of his major league goals said, "As I look back on the times of adversity, I can see that God cared for me, and the adversity or these detours were leading me back to where He wanted me to be."[2]

In God's Word there are some answers—not always specific answers to your circumstances, but general principles that can guide your understanding about the "why" or "why not" of setbacks.

Paul provides insight into God's perspective on setbacks in the book of Romans when he says that, "we also rejoice in our sufferings, because we know that suffering produces perseverance; perseverance, character; and character, hope. And hope does not disappoint us, because God has poured out his love into our hearts by the Holy Spirit, whom he has given us" (Romans 5:3-5).

These verses helped Portland Trail Blazer forward, Buck Williams, deal with adversity in his own life. "My last few years in New Jersey, I held onto those verses. Everyone would always ask me, 'Buck, how can you play so hard when you're not going to win any games?' But through it all, I knew deep in my heart that I was becoming a better person—I was building character. I was also becoming a better basketball player because I was playing on a losing team, which forced me to go out and do more things to help the team"[3]

As you suffer, you will develop perseverance; that quality will deepen your character. Deepened or tested character will result in a hope that God will see you through the setback. God is chiseling out your character through the problems and setbacks you face in athletics.

"This is a tough business we're in, but life's rough and you have to deal with those things," said Denver Bronco Coach Dan Reeves about football. "The main thing is you've got to learn to handle the adversity and realize that the Lord says you're going to develop character through it."[4]

God's purpose in trials is maturity. James 1:4 says, "Perseverance must finish its work so that you may be mature and complete, not lacking anything." Former Dallas Cowboy Coach Tom Landry said, "We develop character by going through adversity. Coaches sometimes talk about a losing year being a 'character-building season,' There's some truth to that, as I've seen from experience."[5]

God also shows his strength through our weakness. Following Cy Young Award winner Orel Hershiser's career-threatening injury he stated, "Having Christ in your life can keep you on an even keel. It helps you go through some fantastic moments like being in the World Series, to supposedly hitting what the world would consider rock bottom in having a career-ending injury. It allows you to continue to be the same person held up by the same God. He shows his might in your weakness."[6] The Apostle Paul said, "My grace is sufficient for you, for my power is made perfect in [weakness]. Therefore I will boast all the more gladly about my weaknesses, so that Christ's power may rest on me" (2 Corinthians 12:9).

How To Rebound from Setbacks

A lot of athletes make excuses when trying to rebound from setbacks. The Dallas Cowboy's place kicker, was asked why he missed a field goal in a game against the Houston Oilers."I was too busy reading my stats on the scoreboard." After he missed another one, he said the stadium's grass was "too tall." In another game he said, "My helmet was too tight and it was squeezing my brain."[7] Once he even blamed Danny White, the holder, for placing the ball upside down.

While some athletes make excuses, others get mad or feel sorry for themselves. None of these responses are helpful. God gives you a better way to rebound from setbacks. Here are some Biblical guidelines for rebounding from setbacks:

1. *Put your trust in God.* According to Proverbs 3:5-6 and other passages, you should put your trust in God and depend on Him. You can choose to rely on yourself, but doesn't it make more sense to place your faith in the one who created you? Just as a head coach is the best person to direct his team, so is God able to guide you through your trials.

Even though it would have been easy for Dave Dravecky to feel sorry for himself after his comeback was cut short by another injury, he continued to trust God. He said, "Sometimes we see God as working in our lives only to bring about our success. But what's more important is the process we go through in the experience. God is watching closely how we respond in that trial or adversity—whether you're going to place your complete trust in Him or not."[8]

Former Philadelphia 76er Bobby Jones, was one of the twelve players on the United States Olympic basketball team in 1972, defending its seven straight Olympic titles. The U.S.S.R. won the gold-medal game in the most controversial finish in Olympic history. The United States team voted to unanimously refuse its silver medal. When Jones was asked about his disappointment years later he said, "Sure, things like that could turn your outlook on life sour. But the longer I am a Christian, the stronger my faith is, and the more I see God working in my life. I see the Lord showing me that what He says is true—that we need to trust Him with all the details of our lives."[9]

2. *Pray and believe God is sufficient*. In the words of the Apostle Paul in Philippians 4:6-7, we are to pray about all of our circumstances, "Do not be anxious about anything, but in everything, by prayer and petition, with thanksgiving, present your requests to God. And the peace of God, which transcends all understanding, will guard your hearts and your minds in Christ Jesus."

"Mean" Joe Green, former All-Pro defensive lineman, is convinced that prayer works. "I had been married for three years. We had a family, and I was trying to get an understanding of how to best deal with all that was before me," Joe said. "Prayer helped give me strength. I think I have a better sense of who I am with prayer. It helps me understand my strength and weakness."[10]

If you could ask God to change one thing in your athletics, knowing that he would grant your requests, would you ask Him...

...to heal your body?
...to give you more playing time?
...to change something about your coach?
...to improve your blocking
...to win more games?
...to improve your team's attitude?

Whatever your request is, do you regularly and diligently, bring it to God in prayer, trusting that He will help you? If not, why not?

God is able. The Bible says it over and over. "Do you not know? Have you not heard? The Lord is the everlasting God, the Creator of the ends of the earth. He will not grow tired or weary" (Is. 40:28). He is able to control nature, alter circumstances, and change people.

No matter what happens in your athletic career, God can supply any of your needs—no matter what.

Woody Hayes, the legendary coach of Ohio State for many years, often told the story of how he came to that giant university to coach football after gaining experience at small schools like Denison and Miami of Ohio. The first time Hayes stood in the middle of the empty OSU stadium he looked at those 86,000 seats and began having second thoughts. Woody's son was holding his hand and must have sensed his father's anxiety over having to try to create teams that could perform successfully before so many fanatical Buckeye followers. With wisdom far beyond his years, the little boy said, "But Daddy, the football field is the same size."[11]

No matter how bad the injury, or how overwhelming the odds are, *the field is still the same size.* And what is more important, the one who made the field is on your side.

Those athletes who rebound from setbacks believe God has the power to do anything, change anyone, and alter circumstances. One athlete who believed God and refused to doubt Him was Andre Thorton.

Andre was the powerful first baseman for the Cleveland Indians. He lost his wife and daughter in a 1977 car accident, but his faith helped him through the difficult days that followed.

Following the accident he kept praying and trusting in God. He said, "My meditation and Bible reading melded into a time of prayer, and the three continued simultaneously. For a while, time seemed suspended as I drew strength from my Lord and from the Scriptures. I prayed that my life would be a testimony for the Lord, even beginning the next morning at the funeral, and that as a result of my faith, others would praise Him."[12]

Jan Ripple, a triathlete, recognizes the importance of God's strength. Jan Said, "Lately I've been wondering how in the world non-Christians can put their bodies through what they do. I don't know how they can put their bodies through that pain threshold without Jesus' help. I can't do any more than what I'm doing. And I couldn't do it without His strength."[13]

3. *Choose to be joyful.* Happiness depends on circumstances, but joy can happen in spite of a difficult situation. Happiness is a feeling, but joy is an attitude. The pain we encounter in life is unavoidable, but misery is optional. You can choose to be joyful.

Outlook determines outcome, and attitude determines action. A joyful attitude is essential when rebounding from setbacks. James says, "Consider it pure joy, my brothers, whenever you face trials of many kinds" (James 1:2).

If you value material and physical things more than spiritual things, then setbacks will upset you. It will be tough for you to "consider it all joy" if you focus only on the past instead of the future. Job, of the Old Testament, had the right perspective when he said, "But he knows the way that I take; when he has tested me, I will come forth as gold" (Job 23:10).

Our faith in Christ helps to give us the proper perspective on setbacks. When Tom Landry was fired from his coaching job with the Dallas Cowboys he said, "It's my faith that allowed me to keep my perspective and not feel devastated or bitter about being fired."[14]

When setbacks come, give thanks to the Lord and adopt a joyful attitude. If it's true that outlook determines outcome, then to end with joy, begin with joy.

4. *Forget the past, focus on the goal.* How do you forget about a fumble or missed spike? How do you forget about striking out when the game is on the line? How can you forget about being badly beaten by your opponent?

During the 1986 American League playoffs, the California Angels had a 3-1 advantage over the Red Sox and a 5-4 lead in the ninth inning of Game Five, and were one strike away from getting into the World Series. Donnie Moore was pitching with a sore right shoulder. Moore threw a ball to Boston's Dave Henderson who hit a two-run homer. Even though the Angels came back to tie the score, Henderson's sacrifice fly off Moore in the eleventh won the game and sparked the Red Sox to two more wins and the A.L. pennant.

After that game, Moore's career, thwarted by injuries, was headed downhill. The Angels released him in 1988 and the Royals cut him in 1989. Finally, in 1989, Moore shot his wife and killed himself. His wife, who survived her wounds, attributed the shooting to his fateful pitch on October 12, 1986. "Henderson's homer was what did it," said David Pintger, Moore's agent. "It sent him over the cliff. He blamed himself for the Angels not going to the World Series. He couldn't get over it."[15]

Moore's inability to cope with his past led to a tragic end. The apostle Paul gives you several practical ways to handle your failures. He wrote, "Brothers, I do not consider myself yet to have taken hold of it. But one thing I do: Forgetting what is behind and straining toward what is ahead, I press on toward the goal to win the prize for which God has called me heavenward in Christ Jesus" (Philippians 3:13-14).

You must learn from the past, but do not be controlled by it. Any runner who looks backward while running forward risks losing the race. The Apostle Paul put his failures behind him and focused on the goal. The goal is to glorify God through your actions.

When you try to rebound from setbacks, try these steps:

a) Forget the past. In Philippians 3:13, Paul used the word "forgetting" which means to forget totally. Paul had to forget about the beatings, shipwrecks, and poverty. You need to forget those things that would keep you from pressing on.

b) Focus on the goal. The word "press" in Philippians 3:14, means to actively go after something. Paul constantly pursued his goal of becoming more like Christ. Paul went beyond just trying to forget a mistake. He understood that by focusing his attention on his goal he could more easily change his behavior.

When Greg Gagne of the Minnesota Twins was asked how he is able to bounce back when he isn't playing well, he said, "Well, It's been tough for me this year. The last four or five errors I've made, they've been scoring two to three runs off the error. And in some ways it's easy to get your eyes on the problems because they're right there in front of you. You play baseball every day, and one day seems to roll into another."

“It’s at those times when I really have to get my focus back on Christ. That’s what helps me to deal with whatever the world is throwing at me, whether it’s my batting average, my errors or strikeouts, or what people think. If my focus isn’t on Christ, then this baseball world is just going to tear Greg Gagne apart. And it’s done that in the past—don’t get me wrong. That’s something that I have to deal with every day.”[16]

c) Fix your eyes on the prize. The winner of the Greek races that Paul had in mind, received a wreath of leaves and sometimes a cash award; the Christian receives an award of everlasting glory. Paul’s ultimate ambitions are found not in this life but in heaven, because Christ is there.

5) Recognize that God is in total control and has a plan for your life. Recognize that God is either causing your circumstance to happen or allowing it to happen for His purpose. God is in total control. Jerry Ediger was injured in a high school football game during his senior year. He dislocated his vertebra in his back and pinched his spinal cord; he was paralyzed from the neck down. Jerry’s perspective on God’s being in control of his situation helped him deal with his setback. “God gave me peace about the whole situation. I’ve been a Christian since I was a little guy. And God let me know he was in control, and everything was going to work out for my good. Just like it says in Romans 8:28. Everything has worked out better than I could have asked for or imagined.”[17] “And we know that in all things God works for the good of those who love him, who have been called according to his purpose” (Romans 8:28).

Bob Wieland is an athlete who understands what Paul had in mind when he talked about God’s sovereign control. He was recruited by the Army during the Vietnam war and was trying to reach an injured soldier when he stepped on the enemy’s hidden 82-millimeter mortar.

He lost both legs and went from a strapping six feet tall and 205 pounds to three feet tall and 87 pounds. Wieland said his faith in God kept him from becoming bitter about losing his legs. "God knows what He is doing, and He had a better plan for my life."[18]

Eight years after the accident, Bob Wieland broke the world bantam weight record by lifting 303 pounds in the bench press, but his record was not allowed because of a technicality. The Amateur Athletic Union disallowed the record because he was not wearing shoes.

The story of Joseph in the book of Genesis describes him losing his status in a wealthy family and being sold by his brothers into slavery. In spite of this, he was able to trust God. He never lost sight of God's ability to keep his promises. "You [his brothers] intended it to harm me, but God intended it for good, to accomplish what is now being done, the saving of many lives" (Genesis 50:20).

Regardless of what has happened to you, recognize that He is in total control of your situation. It doesn't matter how unfair or painful your situation is, God knows—trust Him to use it to bring about His plan for your life.

6) Determination and discipline. Bob Wieland was able to come back from his injury and now tests out at 9.9 percent body fat. Not bad, considering the average American has 20 percent

body fat. But more incredible than that, he walked on his hands across America. His preparation for this feat included 1200 training miles on his hands. His coast-to-coast trip stretched over 2800 miles.

Wieland is a great example of an athlete who was determined to rebound from his circumstances. He said, "Through faith in God, determination and dedication, there is nothing within the will of God a person can't achieve."[19]

Determination is hanging tough when the going gets rough. Athletes often look for short cuts to success, but rebounding from defeat takes hard work. Jesus tells you to "seek first the kingdom of God," the word *seek* implies a strong-minded pursuit. The Greek text of this passage in Matthew means: "Keep on continually seeking..." The idea is determination.

One coach, when asked what made him successful, said that his philosophy could best be summed up by the words written by an anonymous author.

> Press on.
> Nothing in the world
> Can take the place of persistence.
> Talent will not;
> Nothing is more common
> Than unsuccessful men
> With talent.
> Genius will not;
> Unrewarded genius
> Is almost a proverb
> Education will not;
> The world is full of

Educated derelicts.
Persistence and determination
Alone are important.[20]

Discipline is a term that often comes up in testimonies of those who overcome setbacks. Discipline is self-control. The Apostle Paul referred to this in 1 Corinthians 9:25. He said that those who compete in the games exercise "self-control in all things." Discipline is the key.

- No athlete overcomes an injury without it.
- No team improves itself without it.
- No athlete overcomes unfairness without it.

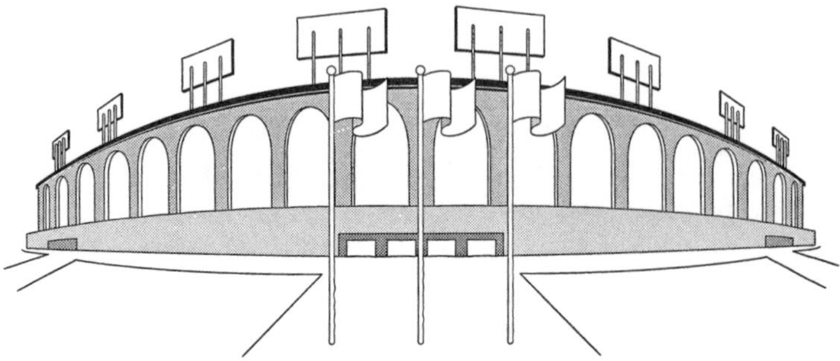

After he graduated from college he was drafted by the Houston Oilers, but he was cut before the season started. They said he was too small and too slow. Eventually, Steve Largent was claimed by an expansion team, the Seattle Seahawks. Against all odds, he set almost every pass receiving record in pro football history. A former teammate, Norm Evans, said, "He's taken his God-given talents and used them to the maximum. Every time he walks off the field he knows he's given it his best."[21]

Steve Largent overcame a setback to use his talent for God, and you can do the same. You may not set records like he did, but you can get the maximum out of your talents by applying determination and discipline to your athletics. You can overcome setbacks!

JUST REMEMBER IT.
"And we know that in all things God works for the good of those who love Him, who have been called according to His purpose" (Romans 8:28).

JUST THINK IT.
I'm going to be better rather than bitter from this experience. I believe that God is either causing my circumstance to happen or allowing it to happen for His purpose. God is in total control.

JUST DO IT.
Take a moment to focus on your goals. Start with your long range goals and work back to what you need to do today to reach them.

JUST PRAY IT.
"Lord, help me to see my situation from your perspective. Thank you for being a God who is in total control of my situation. Help me to grow through this experience. Amen."

HUDDLE DISCUSSION

Setbacks: Turn Setbacks Into Comebacks

LEADING OFF: When you were growing up, what one goal did you want to accomplish most? Why?

1. Where would you position yourself on an optimist-pessimist scale? Why?

2. Setbacks are:

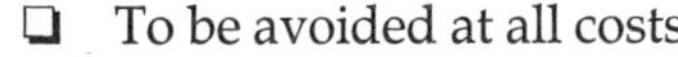

❑ Normal and healthy
❑ To be avoided at all costs

3. What is the worst suffering you've faced as an athlete? What has God taught you through it?

4. What are some recent sports comebacks? (Examples might include: Orel Hershiser, Dave Dravecky, etc.) What has impressed you about these comebacks?

5. For each of the following situations, give your advice.
   a. Bob is depressed because he has just been cut from the team.
   b. Sarah feels like she let the team down last night because she missed the winning shot.
   c. Leslie blew out her knee in practice yesterday and is worried about having surgery and missing the rest of the season.

6. Read each of the Bible verses and then complete the sentences using what you learned from the Bible passage. Be sure to explain the reason you wrote down each sentence.

Romans 5:3-5
When I suffer God is...
Proverbs 3:3-6.
When I'm trying to make a comeback I should...
Philippians 3:13-14
I should try to...
Romans 8:28
When I face trials I know God is...

WIND SPRINTS

Setbacks: Turn Setbacks Into Comebacks

1. How does Romans 5:3-5 relate to setbacks?
2. How can God show His might in our weakness? (See 2 Cor. 12:9).
3. Read Proverbs 3:5-6. What does this passage teach you about athletics and life? Why is it difficult to trust God?
4. How is it possible for Paul to rejoice in the Lord? (See Phil. 4:1). How can you feel joyful about setbacks? (See James 1:2-11).
5. According to Phil. 4:6-7 how can prayer help you overcome a difficult situation?
6. What does it mean to "consider it all joy" in James 1:2? When you encounter problems, is joy a choice or an emotion? Why?
7. What kind of confidence should Romans 8:28 give you in your athletics? How does this relate to the suffering Paul mentions in Romans 8:18?
8. Read Romans 8:29. How does this verse apply to your athletics?
9. What is the source of suffering? (See Romans 5:12). According to the following verses how should you respond to suffering? (1 Peter 2:20-25 and 1 Peter 4:12-14).
10. What is the difference between trials and temptation? (See James 1:1-13).

Do the Right Thing

"Every ethical decision is a decision of the will. We must know what is right and then do it."

CHAPTER 5

CROSS TRAINING MANUAL

ETHICS

"What's the charge, Mulvaney?" "University kid, judge," replied Mulvaney. "Some frat men say he stole their loving cup."

Those were innocent days, the late 1940s, a time when humorist Max Shulman could lightly write about Dobie Gillis getting busted for allegedly swiping Chi Psi's beloved hardware. As the stories about Oklahoma and Colorado on the following pages suggest, today's university kids—the athletes among them, anyway—are more likely to stand accused of rape, assault, break-ins and drug trafficking than they are of Joe College pranks. Coming on top of the widespread under-the-table payments and the academic abuses also associated with big-time intercollegiate sports, the offenses committed by athletes against people and property cast a shadow across American campuses. Loving cups aren't being stolen these days; universities are being robbed of their integrity.[1]

The abuses in sports have even given comics, like Jay Leno, plenty of material. Leno, when commenting on the problems in college athletics said, "Oklahoma's football team has already been ranked 10th in the preseason polls—that's both UPI and FBI."[2]

Times have changed. Competition forces us to make moral choices. Plato believed that he could uncover a person's values more effectively in an hour of play than he could in a year of conversation. Athletes and coaches have their ethics on morality and competition shaped by a society that has rejected Biblical ethics. If this is true, it shouldn't shock us when there are so many problems with moral abuses in athletics.

To make matters worse, our society begins the push toward win at all cost during our youth. As *Sports Illustrated* writer Frank Deford said, we sometimes encourage athletes to make immoral choices:

> When I was in high school we had this big center, about 6-7. In one game we're down by a point with a minute to go. In a melee he's whistled for his fifth foul. Instantly, I shoot up my hand and stomp around and carry on a great act. They give me the foul, he stays in the game, and we win. I wouldn't steal anything at a store, but I stole a foul. After the game the coach congratulated me, saying it was the shrewdest bit of quick thinking he'd ever seen. Off the court I would not have done the same in an equivalent situation. But on the court something immoral and unethical becomes "shrewd play."[3]

Ethics is a word that seems to have lost its meaning in sports. Most athletes and coaches would say they are ethical, despite the degree of integrity found in each of them. Many believe sports build an individual's character, but I believe sports reveal an individual's character.

Every ethical decision is a decision of the will. We must know what is right and then do it. "Anyone, then, who knows the good he ought to do and doesn't do it, sins" (James 4:17).

What is Ethics?

Ethics is defined by Webster as: "The system, or code, of morals of a particular person, religion, group, profession, etc."

Ethics is right thinking about right and wrong. We live in a society where absolutes about right and wrong seem outdated, or irrelevant.

In the midst of an athletic world where winning is everything, and God's laws for day-to-day living are not important, every Christian athlete has a responsibility to follow God's standards.

Making an Impact Through Integrity

Paul Zimmerman, in his book, *A Thinking Man's Guide to Pro Football,* quotes a physicist who made an unbelievable discovery. The physicist had the facts to prove that when a 240-pound lineman (capable of running 100 yards in eleven seconds) collides with a 240-pound running back (capable of covering the same distance in ten seconds), the resultant kinetic energy is "enough to move 66,000 pounds—or thirty-three tons—one inch."

Now that's impact! What about spiritual impact? Are you making an impact on others? Without integrity, forget it. Nothing hurts the credibility of an athlete more than compromising their moral integrity.

Since integrity is so important, there is a great need for Christian athletes and coaches who are known for their integrity. Integrity means different things to different people, but at its core, integrity refers to someone being for real. It means you're not pretending to be something you're not. You are also what you're supposed to be, especially in your ethics

and morals. If someone checks you out, they will find you to be what you said you were.

Integrity can be seen in coaches, like Tom Osborne and Tom Landry. They stand for moral principles and have the courage to stand up for their convictions. When others have looked at their lives they see men who are honest and keep their promises.

In 1990 Coach Tom Osborne turned down a raise from the University of Nebraska. His Athletic Director commented that, "This wasn't the first year Osborne had tried to turn down a raise. We've had trouble trying to get him to take one a couple of other times. Money is important, but to Tom it's not as important as other things in life. He's not a phony. He's a good Christian person, and he has stronger views than money."[4]

For the Christian athlete, integrity means following the same set of values on game day, as you do on Sunday morning at church. Betsy King, professional golfer, understands what it means to compete with Christian values. "Being a Christian has modified her inward character. Betsy's learned to be competitive against the course rather than her opponents. Not long after she had accepted Christ, she was playing in a tournament alongside Laura Baugh. One particular hole was disastrous for Betsy: she twice hit the ball out bounds, taking penalty strokes, and finishing with a 10 on the hole and a 76 for the round. Later in the locker room Laura was overheard saying, "I can't believe Betsy King. She made a 10 out there and didn't get mad!" Although the extra shots were uncharacteristic, Betsy's response was not."[5]

Benefits of Integrity

There are many benefits to athletes who live with integrity. Here are just a few.

1. *Clear conscience.* When you compromise in some area of your life, it's likely that you'll feel guilt. Living a life of integrity rids you of any guilt in your personal life. Jim Wacker, TCU football coach, when faced with rule violations in his program chose not to hide them. "The good thing is you live through it. It's over, and you feel good about it because you did what you believe is right. You draw the line and say this is where we stand and this is what we're going to do. And if you do that, you can look at yourself in a mirror and feel good about yourself."[6]

2. *Motivate others around you to live with integrity.* Whenever you take a stand for what is right, it helps your teammates and others do the right thing. Anthony Munoz, NFL All-Pro, was named to the Playboy magazine All-American team his senior year at the University of Southern California. He refused to be included in a photograph with 40 other top college players and a weekend at a resort. He later joined Cincinnati's Citizens Concerned for Community Values. The group is affiliated with the National Coalition Against Pornography. "If you voice your opinions, things will start to happen," he says. "People listen when you stand up for something."[7]

3. *Close relationship with God.* Since God values integrity, it makes sense that we can become closer to God by living lives

that please Him. Psalm 15 teaches that if we want to be close to God, then we must pursue a morally pure lifestyle. Pitching ace, Orel Hershiser, understands the importance of pleasing God through integrity. In a book on Orel's life, *Grand Slam*, it describes how he learned to say "sorry" to God by confessing sin as soon as he became aware of it. "I wouldn't even wait for my prayers at night. I would just confess at that moment." This habit gave him the assurance of being close to God, and it aided his spiritual growth since sin could not gain a foothold in his life for more than a few moments.[8] One of the benefits of integrity is being able to draw close to God.

4. *Opportunities to be a witness to your teammates.* Many of your teammates will not attend church or other Christian activities. But they will see genuine Christianity up close when they are around you. Brent Jones, San Francisco 49er, realized how important integrity is to his witness when he said, "We're really under the gun. Guys who aren't Christians are taking note of how we react and how we are off the field."[9]

5. *Get the most out of our abilities.* Whether it's sports or school, following spiritual values and not compromising will help you get the most from God's gifts to you. Heisman Trophy winner Barry Sanders was asked how he improved both physically and mentally following his sophomore year in school. "I started to pay attention to spiritual values and how God would want me to live, so I hit the books. Now, the spiritual things are the most important part of my life."[10]

Compromise

Since integrity is so important, why do so many compromise? How many of us have been disappointed by our heroes during the past few years? In baseball it was Pete Rose, Steve Garvey, and Wade Boggs.

In track it was Ben Johnson. During the 1988 Olympic Games he came across the finish line first in the 100-meter dash, but he was using steroids to gain an illegal physical advantage. He compromised his integrity because of the pressure to win at any cost. He was eventually stripped of his gold medal and dishonored in the national press.

A few, like Len Bias and Don Rogers, compromised their values momentarily, and as a result they lost their lives.

When dealing with compromise, it's important to understand that you reap what you sow. Lyle Alzado, former NFL All-Pro, admitted, in an article in *Sports Illustrated,* that he had compromised his health by using steroids: "I lied. I lied to you. I lied to my family. I lied to a lot of people for years when I said I didn't use steroids. I started taking anabolic steroids in 1969, and I never stopped. Not when I retired from the NFL in 1985. Not ever. I couldn't and then I made things worse by using human growth hormone, too. I had my mind set, and I did what I wanted to do. So many people tried to talk me out of what I was doing, and I wouldn't listen. And now I'm sick. I've got cancer—a brain lymphoma—and I'm in the fight of my life."[11]

Why Some Compromise

1. *They flirt with temptation.* People go through several stages when they compromise. First, they start to think about doing wrong; then they imagine what it might be like; and finally they put themselves in a situation where compromise can happen.

2. *They are attracted by flattery and fantasy.* The dictionary defines flattery as "to praise too much, untruly, or insincerely, as in order to win favor." Almost all of athletic temptation involves some flattery. For some athletes who have taken money to play college football or basketball at a certain school, it may have been the flattery of a big time school recruiting him, or the fantasy that they will become well known.

3. *They rationalize their behavior.* The dictionary defines rationalization as "providing possible but untrue reasons for conduct." In other words, it is trying to hide or put up a smoke screen of excuses for doing the wrong thing. Rationalization often gives people an excuse for doing wrong.

Here are just a few rationalizations:

- "They owe it to me!"
- "Who will ever find out?"

- "Everybody does it."
- "It's the way the system works."

It's time athletes called a spade a spade and stopped making excuses. No amount of rationalization will make wrong behavior right.

Satan wants us to believe that no one will find out and there will be no consequences. The athlete who cheats, whether they are doing less in their workout or taking money illegally, tries to convince oneself that there will be no consequences. But there are always consequences.

We will reap what we sow. Even if the NCAA, or our coaches, miss our compromise. It never escapes God. All sin has consequences—they may not come in this life, but they will in the next. Moral compromise always costs.

How to Make The Right Decision

I'm convinced God wants you to know His will. He says, "So then do not be foolish, but understand what the will of the Lord is" (Ephesians 5:17). He is so concerned that you know what to do that He has promised to guide you: "I will instruct you and teach you in the way which you should go; I will counsel you with My eye upon you. Do not be as the horse or as the mule which have no understanding, whose trappings include bit and bridle to hold them in check" (Psalm 32:8-9).

There is not always an easy answer to the issues and problems we face in athletics. Some issues that clearly involve lying or cheating are straightforward. It is the issues that the Bible doesn't directly address that are more complex. How you make decisions today in athletics will determine how you will conduct yourself for the rest of your life in other areas.

There is not an automatic formula for knowing God's will, but there are well-known principles that will guide you in doing the right thing. The guidelines listed here are to help you begin to make decisions correctly.

A Personal Relationship with Jesus Christ

It all starts with a right relationship with Jesus Christ. Before you go any further ask yourself these questions:

1. *Are you a Christian?* If you have never personally asked Jesus Christ to be your Lord and Savior, you cannot expect any of the other guidelines to help.

2. *Are you spending time with God each day through reading the Bible and prayer?* During the season, you wouldn't go for days without listening or talking to your teammates or coaches. Similarly, God wants you to communicate with Him each day.

3. *Are you obeying God and confessing any known sin in your life?* Unless you do what you already know of His will, you can't expect His guidance. To keep your communication open to God, be sure to confess your sin to Him (See 1 John 1:9).

4. *Are you keeping Jesus Christ as your focal point?* Portland Trail Blazer forward Buck Williams has learned how important it is to keep Jesus as the focal point. "You need Jesus Christ as your focal point. For example, everything else around you changes—like I had to change in my life from New Jersey to Portland. In other words, as everything around you changes, you keep your focus on the Lord. As the Bible talks about, "Seek ye first the kingdom of God,..." "and these things will be added unto you" (Matthew 6:33). And that's my way of thinking. Seeking the kingdom of God keeps me focused—which is so important in my life and so important when I walk out on the floor."[12]

Study the Bible

Study the Bible for commands and principles relevant to your decision. It's important to know the Bible and commit yourself to obey it.

While the Bible doesn't speak to every problem you may face in athletics, it does show you the way. You are not going to find anyone in the Bible playing quarterback, but it does give you principles to help you make wise decisions.

David, in Psalm 119:105, had this in mind when he said, "Your word is a lamp to my feet and a light for my path." He also wrote, "Your statutes are my delight; they are my counselors" (Psalms 119:24). The Bible is your light and counselor in a world that is in moral darkness. It reveals to you the correct path to choose. Ask God to use His Word and His Spirit to speak to you.

God's Word is essential to knowing God. J.I. Packer in his fine book, *Knowing God,* said that for many Christians "their basic mistake is to think of guidance as apart from the written Word." The Holy Spirit does speak to us, but always in harmony with God's Word.

Know the Rules

Be aware of the rules that are relevant to your sport. If there are team rules, follow them. If you're being recruited to play college ball, then know what can be promised in recruiting and what cannot. In most cases, you can get a copy of rules and regulations for almost any sport.

Listen to Your Conscience

Your conscience can help you determine what is right and wrong. This is helpful when the Bible does not speak directly to an issue. While you need to be careful not to rely totally on your conscience, it can help you determine early on which way to go. If you're going to use your conscience to help choose right from wrong you must understand what it is and how it works.

"Conscience is that inner knowledge that helps me to know myself."[13] In New Testament days the word "conscience" was used by people to mean "the pain that you feel when you do wrong." Conscience is like having a commentator tell you if your actions are right or wrong.

It's important to understand that your conscience can only properly guide you if you have the right standard. If you cheat on a drill or test, or do something you know you should not do, your conscience bothers you. Something inside you keeps reminding you that you've blown it. That's conscience. For some people, they have abused their conscience to the point that doing wrong doesn't bother them anymore.

Maybe you've heard people say, "Let your conscience be your guide," and to the degree that you depend on God's standards this is good advice. The important thing to remember is to rely on God's standard—the Bible, so that your conscience will work the way He wants it to work. For your conscience to work properly it needs to have the right guide and the right standard to follow.

Get Advice

You can easily lose perspective when trying to make a difficult decision. At times you might need the experience of a more mature Christian. Other Christians might also be able to help with their knowledge of God's Word. "As iron sharpens iron, so one man sharpens another" (Proverbs 27:17).

On spiritual matters, be sure to counsel with Christians. You probably can't live your entire life without the counsel of non-Christians. When the spiritual dimension is involved, the non-Christian is unable to offer godly advice. You can certainly receive good advice on rules and strategies of your sport from a non-Christian. But in areas where spiritual matters are involved, seek out a mature Christian for advice. The Bible says, "How blessed is the man who does not walk in the counsel of the wicked" (Psalm 1:1).

Pray

The Bible promises, "If any of you lacks wisdom, he should ask God, who gives generously to all without finding fault, and it will be given to him" (James 1:5).

Ask God to make you willing to do the right thing. Take time to regularly pray about the details of your decision, and ask for His guidance. Pray with friends and teammates and ask others to pray. (1 Peter 3:12).

It's been said, "Those who walk with God always reach His destination!" I'm convinced that as your prayer life is shaped by God's will, this statement will be true of your life.

Hearing God's Voice

For some people knowing when God is speaking to them is difficult or mysterious. Peter Lord, a minister, wrote in *Fullness* magazine about hearing God's voice. He said he never heard an audible voice, but he thought he could hear the inner voice of God by applying these principles:

1. It did not contradict Scripture.
2. It was not rushed or in a hurry, yet persistent.
3. It was soft, not loud.
4. It was specific and clear.
5. The result would bring glory to Him.
6. It brought peace and not confusion in his own thoughts.

God can speak directly to us or He can even use other people. Most often, though, He speaks to us through His Word.

Someday you will stand before God, and He will evaluate whether or not you have honored Him by making the right decisions about right and wrong. Times have changed. But you need to ask yourself if there is any game, honor or amount of money that is worth the risk of displeasing God. I don't think there is. I hope you'll come to the same conclusion for yourself.

JUST REMEMBER IT.

"Your word is a lamp to my feet and a light for my path" (Ps. 119:105).

JUST THINK IT.

I will honor God's will and values.

JUST DO IT.

Evaluate every moral area of your life. Confess any sin and commit yourself to do the right thing.

JUST PRAY IT.

"Lord, Thank you for your Word. Guide me as I try to obey your Word. Amen."

HUDDLE DISCUSSION

Ethics: Do the Right Thing

LEADING OFF: What is your most embarrassing moment in sports?

Define and discuss the importance of ethics.

Discuss the following statement: "If you don't stand for something, you'll fall for anything."

Who do you think of when you hear the word "integrity"?

One study on athletes showed, that a high percentage of athletes would risk death by taking a drug, if it would help them to perform better than most athletes. Why do you think they would take such a risk?

After twenty years of using steroids, while he was playing football in the NFL, Lyle Alzado became sick with cancer. Why do you think he took steroids? What did he lose because of steroids? What advice would you have given him during his playing days? What advice would you give him now? What do you think about Magic Johnson's announcement about contracting the HIV virus? How should we respond to it?

Kim's basketball team just won the State Championship for the first time in the history of the school. But she has just realized that she was ineligible to play in the championship game. Although she only played during the last 2 minutes, when the game had already been decided, she is not sure if she should say anything to her coach. If she tells her coach, the team will forfeit the game and the championship. If she says nothing, it's unlikely anyone will ever find about the rule infraction. What do you think Kim should do? Why?

Read the following verses and fill in the blanks.
Discuss how each statement is true.
Without integrity the Christian athlete will...

not have a close ________________(Psalm 15).
will hurt his/her ________________(Proverbs15:27).

WIND SPRINTS

Ethics: Do the Right Thing

1. Read James 1:5. According to this verse, how can God's Word help you do the right thing?

2. How can close friends help you keep your ethical edge? (See Proverbs 27:17).

3. According to 1 Peter 1:14-16, why should we watch the way we live our lives?

4. Read Proverbs 7:22-23. What is the cost of moral compromise in this situation?

5. According to Proverbs 10:2 , what is the result of ill-gotten gains?

6. How important is integrity to the Christian athlete? (See Psalm 15, Proverbs 15:27, and Titus 2:9,10).

7. Study each of the following references that deal with integrity: (Genesis 20:6, 1 Kings 9:4, Job 2:3,9, 27:5; 31:6; Psalm 7:8).

8. Read 1 Samuel 24:1-6. What was David's response after he cut off part of Saul's robe?

9. Read Acts 24:16. Why did Paul believe that the conscience needed to be exercised?

10. According to Romans 9:1, when is the conscience a reliable guide?

Teamwork that Works

"God is clear that we need each other, and we need to work together.."

CHAPTER 6

CROSS TRAINING MANUAL

TEAMWORK

"When teamwork kicks in, nobody can beat you." Don Shula, head coach of the Miami Dolphins, who made this comment, knows what he is talking about. Shula has one of the best records in the NFL. When the individual talents on any team blend together they become a powerful force.

Sometimes teamwork comes about through a set of circumstances. The 1989 University of Colorado football team rallied around their cancer-stricken quarterback, Sal Aunese. He was able to watch the first three games of the 1989 season from a private box hooked to an oxygen support system. Sal's teammates wore his name embroidered on their sleeves, and they pointed to him from the field after each big play.

Sal died just before the fourth game of the season. Bill McCartney, Colorado head coach, said, "During the remainder of the season, the team felt Sal's presence. We played as a tight, unified group, winning game after game, ending the season with the Big Eight title, the number-one spot in the national rankings, and an invitation to the Orange Bowl, which had been Sal's dream. Though we lost the bowl game to Notre Dame, we knew we'd had a golden season."[1] He also said that, "The biggest change is not in the overall talent of the team. The biggest change is that this team blended together as one ... Sal helped us do that more than any other guy. Sal was team. That's the legacy he left behind."[2]

When teams don't work together, it's not only difficult to win, but it's also tough for teammates to play together.

When star running back Eric Dickerson finally returned to his team after financial problems with the Colts in 1990, his problems had an impact on the entire team. *Sports Illustrated* reported that his teammates weren't waiting for him with open arms at the door of the locker room. Inside were the guys he ripped during his training camp holdout. "He's definitely burned some bridges," said quarterback Jack Trudeau. "Time will be needed to repair them."[3]

Importance of Teamwork

God has a lot to say about teamwork. In the Bible it says:

"Two are better than one because they have a good return for their labor" (Eccles. 4:9).

"For where two or three are gathered in my name, there am I in the midst of them" (Matthew 18:20).

"The Lord God said, "It is not good for the man to be alone" (Genesis 2:18).

The Bible is full of examples of teamwork. Two obvious examples are the Trinity, and Jesus and His team of disciples. Very few, if any, people in the Bible accomplished anything on their own.

God is clear that we need each other, and we need to work together. In fact, it is so important that when Jesus taught us how the world would know his disciples, he gave us two ways. First, "by bearing much fruit" and secondly by obeying his new commandment, "loving each other ... even as he has loved us" (John 15:8; 13:34). Teamwork is what makes love possible. Our working together is important to God!

A team of athletes working together can accomplish much more than the separate members working individually. That's what "synergy" is. The word *synergy* means that "the sum total is greater than the total of the separate parts." It's the idea of working together. Some people have estimated that if you could get all the muscles in your body to pull in one direction, you could lift over twenty-five tons. In Buckminster Fuller's book, *Synergetics*, he believes that "one plus one can equal four if we put our efforts together in the same direction."

Training specialist, John Noe, believes teamwork can accomplish amazing things, if we learn to work together the way our body parts do. He trained for two years by running the back roads of Indiana to prepare himself to scale the 14,780 -foot Matterhorn of Switzerland.

> As Noe worked out to prepare for the climb, he looked down at his feet and said, "One day these feet are going to stand on top of the Matterhorn!" When he made his climb to the summit, he was constantly aware of how his body parts worked as a team. His feet found solid foot holes as his hands grabbed at the edges of the sharp rock. His legs and arms lifted his weight as his heart and lungs worked to pump oxygen from the thin air.

> After he made it to the top, he took a photograph of himself with his feet standing on the Matterhorn. The picture has special meaning, says Noe, "Only because my feet were attached to me."[4]

John Noe's example of what body parts can do together to climb a mountain shows what teamwork can accomplish.

Things that Divide a Team

Possibly the greatest danger to any team or church is individualism. This type of person says, "What's in it for me?", rather than, "What can I contribute to the team?" The Bible deals with the dangers of selfishness, which leads to a lack of teamwork. It's interesting that the Bible refers to Christians as the "body" of Christ. From a physiological perspective, every cell in the body is made for every other cell. The purpose of each cell is to allow all the other cells to perform. The only cell that exists for itself is a cancer cell.

There are at least three types of cancer cells that affect any team. Teams that lack teamwork are ambitious, proud, and self-centered. The Apostle Paul in Philippians 2:3,4, lists these three reasons why we don't work together. Paul says we should "do nothing out of selfish ambition or vain conceit, but in humility, consider others better" than ourselves. Each Christian should look not only to his or her own interests, but also to the interest of others (vv. 3,4).

Nothing is wrong with ambition, unless you become greedy and selfish from being too ambitious. Obviously, God doesn't want you to be lazy, but too much ambition that becomes selfish can hinder the overall team performance. Almost every coach has at one time or another benched a player who wasn't playing for the team. A basketball player too concerned with his scoring average might pass up opportunities to pass the ball to his teammates and begin to force shots.

When Paul talked about vain conceit—he had in mind those people who were out to impress others. Vain conceit means "empty glory," and was probably the root cause of selfish ambition. Athletes who try to do it all themselves are often called "glory hogs". They are only concerned with seeing their name in the headlines. They crave the attention that comes from being in the spotlight. Focus too much on yourself and you neglect your teammates. If you neglect your teammates it will result in division and ultimately have a negative impact on your team performance.

The Buffalo Bills learned a valuable lesson about unity during the 1989 season. They were labeled the "Bickering Bills" because of their frequent disagreements among teammates. A couple of teammates even went on a talk show to try to settle their differences. The bickering eventually hurt the Bills, who were one of the most talented football teams. The division led to a disappointing 9-7 season. In 1990 they finally ended their bickering and recorded the second best regular season record of 13-3. They went on to lose the Super Bowl to the Giants by a narrow margin.

Teambuilding

When the Colorado football team rallied around their ill team leader they pulled together as a unit. This sense of community and cohesiveness doesn't just happen by itself. While circumstances might pull your team together at times, it won't consistently build a spirit of commitment. If any team expects to play up to their potential they need to be concerned about the attitudes and actions of their teammates. Using the acronym, T-E-A-M, here are some practical ways you can do your part to build teamwork.

TEAM

Time Spent Together

You can't build a solid relationship unless you spend time together. It's just not possible to show up for the games as strangers and play together as a team. When you spend time together with your teammates it shows you're interested in what they feel and think.

One of the key ingredients to the best sports teams in history has been time spent together. That's one reason veteran teams have an advantage over expansion teams. The expansion teams may have equal or even greater talent, but they have not spent enough time playing together as a unit. I heard Charles Barkley of the Philadelphia 76ers say it took him at least a full year to adjust to a new point guard when they lost Maurice Cheeks. The great sports teams that built dynasties like the Steelers in football, the Celtics in basketball, and the Yankees in baseball were all veteran teams.

Jesus spent three years with the disciples. Their cohesiveness and team spirit probably wouldn't have been possible without the time they spent together. The result of their teamwork is history. No team has ever had a greater impact on the world then Jesus Christ and his disciples.

Encourage Your Teammates

What you say to your teammates can dramatically affect team attitude.

Paul says, "Do not let any unwholesome talk come out of your mouths, but only what is helpful for building others up according to their needs, that it may benefit those who listen" (Ephesians 4:29). Sometimes even the things you might joke about could be considered unwholesome talk. Sarcasm can easily get out of hand in a lockeroom. I knew a group of

athletes that came up with a way to keep unwholesome talk to a minimum. When the joking got out of hand, they would tell their teammate that their remark was a "4:29". This was a reminder that Ephesians 4:29 condemns unwholesome talk.

Be an encourager. Paul says, "Therefore encourage one another and build each other up" (1 Thessalonians 5:11). There is no doubt that positive feedback builds us up and improves athletic performance. That's probably why most teams prefer to play at home. The home field advantage is common in most sports. It is an advantage to the home team when the crowd gets excited about a play and begins to cheer as it really pumps the team up.

You need to encourage your teammates. Here are a few suggestions on how you can encourage your teammates:

• *Build teammates up with positive words.* Call out their name if they make a good play. If they blow it, reassure them that it's only temporary. Be as specific and natural as you can. Don't flatter them— just be honest. Let your teammates know you appreciate them! "Oil and perfume make the heart glad, So a man's counsel is sweet to his friend" (Proverbs 27:9).

• *High-Five, or handskake.* This includes whatever kind of handshake or sign you do after a big play.

• *Smile.* Don't paste on a fake smile! Be yourself, but don't walk around with a frown on your face. It's encouraging when people smile and give us positive feedback. "When a King's face brightens, it means life; his favor is like a rain cloud in spring" (Proverbs 16:15).

Assist Your Teammates

There are at least two ways you can assist your teammates in order to build teamwork.

1. *Play your role.* Any football player knows it's important to carry out his assignments. When I played defensive end, my coaches drilled into me that I needed to "stay at home" when the play went away from me. That's not easy when you seem to be missing all the fun, but if the other team runs a reverse you'd better be waiting for it.

Each player on the team must also carry out their assignment. Without this team unity very few teams will have any success. Imagine what would happen to a football team where everyone wants to play quarterback. The team doesn't need eleven quarterbacks. There must be diversity among the players. The offense needs ends, guards, tackles, backs, and a center.

When the ministry of Jesus was becoming more popular than that of John the Baptist, rather than being jealous of Jesus, he said, "He must become greater; I must become less" (John 3:30). John clearly understood his role was to support Jesus by helping prepare the way for Jesus' ministry.

Paul teaches the Corinthian Church the need for unity combined with the diversity of different gifts in 1 Corinthians 12. I think it's also a great illustration of how important diversity and unity are to teamwork.

"The body is a unit, though it is made up of many parts; and though all its parts are many, they form one body. So it is with Christ. For we were all baptized by one Spirit into one body—whether Jews or Greeks, slave or free—and we were all given the one Spirit to drink. Now the body is not made up of one part but of many. If the foot should say, "Because I am not a hand, I do not belong to the body," it would not for that reason cease to be part of the body. And if the ear should say, "Because I am not an eye, I do not belong to the body," it would not for that reason cease to be part of the body. If the whole body were an eye, where would the sense of hearing be? If the whole body were an ear, where would the sense of smell be? But in fact God has arranged the parts in the body, every one of them, just as he wanted them to be. If they were all one part, where would the body be? As it is, there are many parts, but one body. The eye cannot say to the hand, "I don't need you!" And the head cannot say to the feet, "I don't need you!" On the contrary, those parts of the body that seem to be weaker are indispensable, and the parts that we think are less honorable we treat with special honor. And the parts that are unpresentable are treated with special modesty, while our presentable parts need no special treatment. But God has combined the members of the body and has given greater honor to the parts that lacked it, so that there should be no division in the body, but that its parts should have equal concern for each other"
(1 Corinthians 12:12-25)

In the above passage, the eyes, the hands, and the feet are just as important as the head of the body. If you sit on the bench, you may feel like the feet. But you are just as important as those who are playing.

The person sitting on the bench may find it difficult to accept that role. It doesn't mean being satisfied sitting on the bench. It means accepting the role and being prepared to play. When I played college football, my coach often pointed to the importance of the scout squad. The scout squad rarely gets any recognition, but without them the first team can't properly prepare for the game. If the scout squad doesn't accurately portray the opposing team, then the first team can't get a good picture of what to expect on game day.

An important lesson from this illustration is that you should respect each member of the team regardless of position. All positions on the team are important to the success of the team. Each member of the team needs to be content with a role on the team and work in harmony with the rest of the members. The more you understand how God wants to use you in your sport, the more you'll be able to see how important your role is.

2. *Look out for the best interest of your teammates.* Since selfish ambition, vain conceit, and self-centeredness tear down team unity, looking out for your teammates' interest brings unity. The unselfish athlete doesn't use words like, "I", "me," "my," and "mine." Humility is what makes this possible. "In humility, consider others better than yourselves. Each of you should look not only to your own interests, but also to the interests of others" (Phil. 2:3,4).

The greatest contrast between the selfish and the unselfish athlete that I've seen recently happened on May 1, 1991. The A's Rickey Henderson finally got his record breaking stolen base No. 939, and at the same time 44-year old Nolan Ryan pitched his seventh no-hitter.

Following the no-hitter, a humble Ryan expressed his appreciation for the home town fans. He was thankful that he could do it in front of them. After the game he did his usual 30 minute work out.

By contrast, following Henderson's record theft, during the fourth inning of the game, he lifted the base in the air and paraded around the field. Lou Brock, the previous record-holder, briefly congratulated him. Then Henderson proclaimed, "Lou Brock was a great base stealer, but today I am the greatest of all time."[5]

True humility does not mean you tear yourself down to build someone else up. The humble athlete does not raise himself up and try to put himself above others.

A poem written by Aileen Myers that expresses true humility is Cr*edit Another*.

I made the score,
But don't give me the credit.
Give the credit
to the player who blocked off
the opponent,
to the teammate who threw
within reach,
to the untiring coach who
taught me skills,
to God who gave me
Countless abilities.[6]

In 1 Corinthians 13 the word *love* occurs throughout. Many people think of love only in the romantic sense, but here in the Bible it has a different meaning. It means you should strive for the best interests of others. Love is crucial to effective teamwork.

The Apostle Paul in 1 Corinthians 13:1-3 explains the importance of love. I've summarized his conclusions along with an athletic paraphrase.

Without love...

...my words are empty.
...my speeches and interviews mean nothing.

...my life is empty.
...my games and practices are empty.

...my gains are empty.
...my trophies, championships, and money will count for nothing.

How to Assist Your Teammates

1 Corinthians provides a list of principles on how you can seek your teammates best interests. Applying these principles will create a climate for teamwork to grow and develop.

Be patient (1 Cor. 13:4a). Real love doesn't have a short fuse. No matter how unfair or mean your teammates get, you need to be slow to anger.

Be kind (1 Cor. 13:4a). You need to be helpful to your teammates. Even if it means helping someone who plays your position, you need to be helpful. Being kind means being slow to criticize or condemn.

Don't be jealous (1 Cor. 13:4b). Don't burn with envy for the person who seems to get more attention or play ahead of you. Being an offensive lineman on a football team isn't always easy. They are often overlooked and seldom appreciated for their efforts. Even if your circumstance is lousy, you need to be glad for your teammates' abilities and opportunities.

Don't brag (1 Cor. 13:4b). Boasting only creates problems between teammates. It doesn't mean you can't receive recognition and awards, but when you do it, do it without drawing undue attention to yourself.

Don't be arrogant (1 Cor. 13:4c). Don't strut around with an inflated ego. Don't look down or cut down your teammates who haven't accomplished what you have.

Don't be rude (1 Cor. 13:5a). If you care about your teammates you will do and say the right thing at the best time in a tactful way.

Don't be selfish (1 Cor. 13:5a). Successful teams understand the need for unselfish players. When players demand that their interests come first they cause others to feel resentful. Teamwork needs self<u>less</u> individuals who are willing to give up their own interests when it will benefit others.

The 1991 Chicago Bulls are a great example of a team that was willing to put aside their own self interests for the team. Before winning the NBA Championship against the Lakers, Michael Jordan was considered one of the best players to ever play basketball. One of the few things he had not accomplished was to be a part of a championship team. During the series against the Lakers, he continued to score points, but he involved his teammates more by passing up shots he might otherwise have taken himself. The Bulls swept the Lakers in

Los Angeles. Jordan's selfless play played an important part of the impressive win by the Bulls.

Don't get angry (1 Cor. 13:5b). A person who cares about their teammates is not easily angered. Don't become irritated with your teammates and let bitterness creep into your relationship.

Don't hold onto anger (1 Cor. 13:5c). Don't mentally hold onto resentment toward a teammate because of something he's done. Forgive them for what they've done.

Don't take pleasure when others have done wrong (1 Cor. 13:6a). When one of your teammates breaks the rules, you should feel sorrow for his wrongdoing.

*Be truthful with your teammates (*1 Cor. 13:6b). Be honest and open. This isn't always easy, but it's better to hurt a teammate a little now than have them hurt more later. "Faithful are the wounds of a friend, But deceitful are the kisses of an enemy" (Proverbs 27:6).

*Support your teammate*s (1 Cor. 13:7a). Even if your teammates let you down, support them. Real love is able to survive even if your teammate blows it. Your friendship for them should not be fickle or conditional.

Trust your teammates (1 Cor. 13:7b). You don't need to be gullible, but don't be suspicious and cynical. Give your teammates the benefit of the doubt.

Expect and look for the best in your teammates (1 Cor. 13:7b). Be confident that God has the ability to change them.

Stand tough with your teammates (1 Cor. 13:7). Keep going

no matter what the odds. Refuse to quit. Don't give up on your teammates.

Maintain Team Spirit

The team that works to maintain team spirit has that extra spark to keep it united. There are at least two ways to maintain team spirit.

1. *Respect your coaches.* Respect for authority is critical to team spirit. Without a chain-of-command concept of authority, there is confusion. The chain-of-command is a biblical concept that God gives us so we can function.

On a basketball team, the chain-of-command is the head coach followed by the assistant coaches and then the players.

In 1 Peter it says, "Servants be submissive to your masters with all respect ... for this finds favor with God" (1 Peter 2:18-20). It may be difficult to respect a coach who doesn't act like he deserves your respect, but you are responsible to follow his lead. Your attitude toward him, or her, will greatly impact how your team works together.

Being respectful and submitting to your coach's directives doesn't mean you have to be a doormat. Jesus demonstrated how to handle a situation where there is a difference of opinion. While Jesus was in the Garden of Gethsemane he fell on the ground in agony. He prayed, "Everything is possible for you. Take this cup from me. Yet not what I will, but what You will" (Mark 14:36).

Jesus was asking the Father if there was a different plan other than for Him to endure the painful crucifixion and to be separated from His Father. On a similar note but in a much smaller scale, it might be like an athlete asking his coach if there was any way to run a different play than the one given.

Jesus expressed His feelings, but was willing to do whatever the Father wanted. As an athlete you have the right to go to your coach and express yourself in an appropriate way, but you need to be committed ultimately to follow his or her decision.

2. *Forgive and forget your teammates' mistakes.* Everybody blows it sooner or later. If you don't believe it, take a look at one of the NFL football blooper films. These films show pro athletes who run the wrong way, drop simple passes, and fall on their faces. If a pro athlete can make mistakes with the best of motives, so can your teammates.

The principal of forgiveness is found in Ephesians 4:31-32, which says:

"Let all bitterness and wrath and anger and clamor and slander be put away from you, along with all malice. And be kind to one another, tender-hearted, forgiving each other, just as God in Christ also has forgiven you. The idea is that you are to forgive others "... as God in Christ also has forgiven you."

Jesus made it clear to Peter that forgiveness is a way of life. " 'Lord, how many times shall I forgive my brother when he sins against me? Up to seven times?' Jesus answered, 'I tell you not seven times, but seventy-seven times' "
(Matthew 18:21-22).

In addition to forgiving, it is important to forget. Don't fume about your teammates' mistakes. Forgetting means:

- Refusing to keep track of their mistakes.
- Don't keep score (1 Cor. 13:5).
- Be bigger than the offense (Ps. 119:165).
- Refuse to hold onto any judgmental attitude (Matt. 7:1-5).

In other words, remembering God's perspective involves overlooking your teammates' mistakes.

There is no doubt that the power of teamwork can multiply the performance of your team. Not all your teammates may be Christians, but as you act in their best interest, God will provide you an important opportunity to earn the right to share your faith.

JUST REMEMBER IT.
"Therefore encourage one another and build each other up, just as in fact you are doing."
(1 Thessalonians 5:11).

JUST THINK IT.
I need to encourage and assist my teammates.

JUST DO IT.
During your next practice or game, select one teammate to encourage with a positive word.

JUST PRAY IT.
"Lord, Thank you for the opportunity to be a part of your team. Help me to be a good witness to my teammates for your sake. Amen."

HUDDLE DISCUSSION

Teamwork: Teamwork that Works

LEADING OFF: What was your favorite team when you were growing up? Why?

What is the first thing you think about when you hear the word "teamwork"? Why?

What is the best example of teamwork you can think of?

When former Minnesota Twins Gary Gaetti became a Christian, his close friend and teammate Kent Hrbek resented his change in attitude and behavior. Is it always possible to maintain team spirit when others see a teammates religion as an intrusion? Why or why not?

How should you respond to a teammate who...

a. ...is letting his or her press clippings go to their head.
b. ...just missed the game winning shot.
c. ...was just benched because of a poor attitude.
d. ...was demoted to second string.

Jim's football coach always seems to pick on him. Jim is fed up with his coach, but doesn't know what to do. To make matters worse, his coach claims to be a Christian. Jim feels like he is being unjustly treated and that his coach is a hypocrite. What advice can you give him?

9. Rate your team from 1 to 10 on the scales below by placing an X on the place that best describes your team.

Division——————————————Unity

What are some examples of teamwork in the Bible? Be sure to explain how teamwork helps in each case.

Study the following passages of scripture and discuss how it relates to teamwork.
1 Thessalonians 5:11 • 1 Corinthians 12 • 1 Corinthians 13

WIND SPRINTS

Teamwork: Teamwork that Works

1. Read Matthew 18:20, Eccles. 4:9, and Genesis 2:18. What does the Bible say about teamwork?

2. What does the word *synergy* mean? Why is it important?

3. What are the reasons for living in unity according to Phil. 2:1?

4. Read 1 Thessalonians 5:11. How can you encourage your teammates?

5. According to 1 Peter 2:18-20 what kind of relationship should you have with your coaches?

6. Read Ephesians 4:31-32. How should you respond to a teammate who blows it?

7. Read 1 Cor. 13:5, Ps. 119:165, and Matt. 7:1-5. According to these verses, what does forgiveness mean?

8. Read 1 Corinthians 12. How does this chapter apply to teamwork?

9. How important is love in developing teamwork? (See 1 Cor. 13).

10. What does Romans 13:1-5 teach about authority? How does this apply to your relationship to your coaches?

Get Into Spiritual Shape

"Just as getting into physical shape requires discipline and hard work, so does getting into spiritual shape."

CHAPTER 7

CROSS TRAINING MANUAL

CROSS TRAINING PART 1

Physical exercise has always been important to me. While playing college football, I quickly became aware of the benefits of being in shape for the season. I also found out what kind of effort and pain was involved in getting into shape. I discovered first hand what the saying, "No pain, no gain", meant.

Just as getting into physical shape requires discipline and hard work, so does getting into spiritual shape. A person doesn't just automatically happen to develop spiritually apart from discipline any more than an athlete automatically develops strong muscles.

The Apostle Paul said we are to train or discipline ourselves to be godly (1 Timothy 4:7). Paul also said, "Everyone who competes in the games goes into strict training" (1 Corinthians 9:25). If an athlete trains himself to get a prize that is temporary, he said, how much more should we as Christians discipline ourselves to receive a crown that lasts forever.

Athletes cannot expect to perform well in an athletic contest unless they have adequately worked out to get their bodies into shape. Christians who want to glorify God by their actions need to be spiritually prepared when put to the test.

We grow spiritually as we become more and more like Christ. Our lives are increasingly directed by the Holy Spirit as we commit ourselves to obey his Word. By following basic spiritual disciplines we allow God to work in our lives. They help build our faith.

Many great athletes use cross-training or multiple activities to achieve total physical fitness. In a similar way, the *Cross Training Workout* offers various spiritual disciplines to achieve total spiritual fitness.

In order to get the most out of this book, you should get the *Cross Training Workout*. Throughout the next two chapters there will be many references to it. These next two chapters cover several spiritual disciplines, but you'll need the *Cross Training Workout* to record your progress in these disciplines. A description and ordering information of the *Cross Training Workout* is in the Appendix on page 159.

The important thing in each of the spiritual disciplines is to realize that each is not a thing or a feeling, but a relationship with God that is developing. Each of these disciplines involves a commitment to God that involves getting to know Him better, so that the more deeply we know Him the more fully we can love Him, and the more fully we love Him, the more we can serve Him.

Training Tips

1. *Tap into the power source.* Spiritual growth doesn't just happen by human effort alone. If you depend on yourself, forget it! That's like a high school girl's volleyball team trying to beat the San Francisco 49er's in a football game. Once you've committed yourself to Jesus Christ you have a new source of power available—the Holy Spirit. The Christian life is Jesus Christ living His life through you by the Power of the Holy Spirit.

a. Who is the Holy Spirit?
The Holy Spirit is the third person of the Trinity. He is fully God and a Person.

b. What does the Holy Spirit do?
Jesus Christ was a Helper, Counselor, Strengthener, and Supporter to His disciples. When He returned to His Father, He sent the Holy Spirit to fill those roles for us (John 14:16).

The Holy Spirit:

- ✓ Reveals to us who Jesus is
- ✓ Convicts us of sin
- ✓ Gives us understanding about God's Word
- ✓ Recalls God's Word to our mind
- ✓ Transforms us into Christ's spiritual and moral likeness

2. *Train with teammates.* Accountability is important to the success of every athlete. When I played college football, weight lifting was mandatory. In fact, everyone dreaded the thought of the weight circuit during winter conditioning. It was a gruelling workout with a number of different weight machines. The objective was to go as fast as we could go. Vomiting was common and survival seemed unsure.

Believe it or not, the workouts were exactly what we needed. Most of us even agreed that this was what we wanted. Everyone wanted to become a great athlete, but on our own we would never have worked hard enough to make it happen.

The accountability of having a weight coach who supervised us was important. He helped us to become more than we could have been by ourselves. He got behind us and pushed us toward our goals.

Spiritually it's also natural to follow the path of least resistance. Our goal is to become like Jesus Christ, so doesn't it make sense to use all the resources or tools available?

Find a friend who will help keep you accountable to each of the spiritual disciplines in this chapter. Discipline is never easy, but it's usually worth the price you pay. "Iron sharpens iron, so one man sharpens another" (Proverbs 27:17).

Back to the Basics

The late football coach, Vince Lombardi, was known for his attention to fundamentals. Time and time again he would come back to the basic techniques of blocking and tackling. Once his team, the Green Bay Packers, lost to an inferior team. He didn't like losing, much less losing to a team that had less talent. Coach Lombardi called a team meeting the next morning. His championship team sat silently fearing what he might say to them.

Looking around at each of his players he began:

"Ok, we go back to the basics this morning..."

Holding a football high enough for all to see, he continued to yell:

"... gentlemen, *this* is a *football!*"

That's pretty basic! Especially for a seasoned coach to talk like that to a group of professional athletes. Lombardi believed in a simple philosophy. He thought that excellence could be achieved by perfecting the basics of the sport.

What works in football works in the Christian life. It's easy to get away from the basics of the Christian life. Prayer, Bible

study, and scripture memory are all basic. But each is essential for spiritual growth.

If I were speaking to a struggling group of Christians I might start with:

"Folks, *this* is a *Bible!*"

This chapter will take you back to the basics of the Christian life. Each step takes discipline.

JUST READ IT.

Why read the Bible? God's primary way of communicating with us is through the Bible. The written words of the Bible are "God-breathed"—that's what *inspired* in 2 Timothy 3:16 literally means. It's not enough to read a lot of books about the Bible. There is no substitute for reading Scripture.

The Bible tells us:

- Who God is.
- What God wants.
- What God offers.

The Bible will also help us:

- Grow spiritually.
- Keep us from sin.
- Know God's will.

What is the Bible? The Bible was written by over forty authors in two main languages over a 1,600-year period. The book is inspired by God, so each writer from every walk of life, including kings, peasants, poets, statesmen, scholars, and fishermen, was inspired by God to create one message.

The Bible is made up of the Old and the New Testament. The Old Testament was written before Jesus was born, while the New Testament was written after He died and rose again. They are called the Old and New Testaments because of the agreements between God and man before and after the death of Christ.

The Old Testament is a contract or agreement between God and Israel. During Old Testament times the people were to follow the laws that God had given Moses. In the agreement, God would bless and protect the people if they obeyed the laws. If they didn't obey the laws and sinned, there was a system of animal sacrifices that would "cover" their sin. The blood of an innocent animal covered the sin of that person.

The New Testament came about when Jesus Christ was put to death on a cross as a sacrifice. Jesus became the perfect, innocent sacrifice, while the animal sacrifice only covered the peoples' sin from God's eyes. Jesus' sacrifice actually took the sin away, or paid the penalty for sin. Under the new agreement we don't have hundreds of laws to worry about, but instead we have God Himself, in the Holy Spirit, living inside us. It's now our faith in Christ, not how closely we can follow all the laws, that makes us righteous in God's eyes.

The Bible is more than a history book, because it is God's love letter to us. When you read it, think of it not so much as another textbook, but read it the way you would read a letter from someone who loves you. I'm sure you get more excited about receiving a love letter from your girlfriend, boyfriend, or spouse than reading a history assignment.

The Goal of Bible Reading

The Bible was not written to satisfy our intellectual curiosity, but to change our lives. The goal of Bible reading is not to do something to it, but to have it do something to us. The better we understand God's Word, the more like Jesus Christ our lifestyle should become. Our responsibility is not just to get into the Bible, but to get the Bible into us.

Guidelines for Reading the Bible

I. *Read it daily.* It's important to set aside time to read the Bible each day. The Bereans searched "the Scriptures daily" (Acts 17:11). Just as eating is important to physical health, regular time spent in God's Word is necessary for your spiritual health.

The *Cross Training Workout* will take you through the entire Bible in one year and through the Gospels twice during the year. If you find it difficult to keep pace with the amount of reading, you might want to stick with the New Testament reading until you can add the Old Testament reading. It's better to set aside twenty minutes every day than to try to read for an hour a day but to fail most of the time. Start with an amount of time you can consistently spend each day. There is a spot for recording your own Scripture reading plan. If you're using a daily devotional and don't want to give it up, you can still use the *Cross Training Workout* for recording what God is teaching you.

Think about how much time you spend reading magazines or the newspaper. Most people are capable of sitting down and reading the Bible for at least ten or fifteen minutes a day. It may take time to develop a taste for God's Word, but it's worth it. Find a quiet place away from distractions when you read your Bible. It also helps to set aside a specific time each day to read.

I personally have found that early mornings work best for me. Once the day gets going, it's hard for me to slow down and concentrate on reading the Bible. It seems as if all of the

distractions and pressures of the day keep me from focusing on Scripture. No matter what time of day you read, keep that time the same. Most of us are creatures of habit. Just as a set time helps get you into the proper mind-set when you physically work out, so it will help you in your devotional life.

Be sure to start your reading time by asking God to help you get the most out of your time in the Word. The psalmist prayed,

> "Open my eyes that I may see wonderful things in your law." (Psalm 119:18)

Knowing what to look for when you are reading will help you understand God's Word. Many people struggle with this because they're not taught how to observe the text when they read. How can an experienced detective spot clues that others miss? He has been trained in observation.

By training yourself to observe the text by asking the right questions, you can better understand what you read. While these six questions are basic, they are still helpful because they will force you to observe the text.

1. Who? Who are the personalities in the passage you are reading? What do these people say? What is said about them?

2. What? What is happening?

3. When? When did this take place?

4. Where? Where did this take place?

5. Why? Why is this included in Scripture?

6. How? How did it happen?

Each week the *Cross Training Workout* lists these six questions to encourage you to ask them as you read Scripture.

II. Reflect on it. First Read the Bible, then spend some time meditating on it. "Do not let this book of the Law depart from your mouth; meditate on it day and night, so that you may be careful to do everything written in it" (Joshua 1:8). Meditation is digesting a Scriptural truth by chewing on it over and over until you understand it and know how to apply it to your life. It's letting God's Word sink into your heart.

According to Proverbs 23:7, you become what you think about. Since this is true, the more time you spend meditating on God's Word, the greater the chance for spiritual growth in your life.

III. Record it. One of the best things you can do is record what God has taught you from His Word. Writing down what you've learned not only creates a permanent record, but it also helps you understand the passage.

The *Cross Training Workout* gives you space to record your Bible reading highlights. These might include: the main point or theme of the passage, any questions or problems in the passage, observations and special feelings, or any other thoughts you may have. There is also space for your personal application.

IV. Respond to it. The Word of God should be changing your life. It's more important that God's Word has been through you, than how often you've been through it. It's important to apply the Bible to your life.

Bible Study Resources

To play basketball, you need a basketball. To play baseball you need a bat. If you want to get the most out of the Bible you need the right tools. I've listed several resources that can help you better understand what you read in the Bible. Let me caution you! Do your own study first. Then consult the Bible resources.These resources should help you answer difficult questions and provide valuable background information. But don't let them take the place of your own study.

Bible Translation. The most important resource for Bible reading and study is the Bible itself. And the best way to understand it is to read it consistently. Choosing an accurate, yet understandable translation of the Bible will help you understand what you are reading. *The New International (NIV)* or *New American Standard (NASB)* are considered two of the best. *The King James Version* uses hard-to-understand language, but you may feel more comfortable using it. You may find the "Parallel Bibles" helpful. They have several translations of the same text side by side. Reading several translations can help give you new insights into verses. A paraphrase Bible, like *The Living Bible,* shouldn't be used as your primary version for study. It is helpful for general reading and as a commentary on the text.

Study Bibles. Study Bibles are useful for providing the background information on people, places, events and doctrines.

They will give you the necessary information to understand each book of the Bible. At the beginning of each book, there will be an introduction giving the book's background, author, date, and message. Also included are cross-references and comments in the margins. Several good Study Bibles are *The NIV Study Bible* (Published by Zondervan), *The Ryrie Study Bible* (Moody), and *The Harper Study Bible* (Zondervan).

Bible Dictionary. This is an excellent reference tool. Like the study Bibles, it provides background information on people, places, events and doctrines. Two good bible dictionaries are *The New Bible Dictionary* (Tyndale) *and The Harper's Bible Dictionary* (Harper & Row).

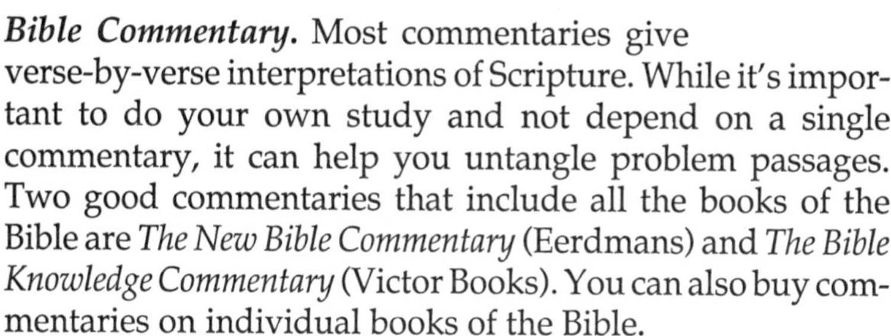

Bible Commentary. Most commentaries give verse-by-verse interpretations of Scripture. While it's important to do your own study and not depend on a single commentary, it can help you untangle problem passages. Two good commentaries that include all the books of the Bible are *The New Bible Commentary* (Eerdmans) and *The Bible Knowledge Commentary* (Victor Books). You can also buy commentaries on individual books of the Bible.

Bible Study Guides. Good study guides help ask questions and structure your reading for you. Some study guides deal with specific topics or single books of the Bible. Some guides are for individual study, while others are for small groups. Two good ones are L*ifeChange* (NavPress) *and LifeGuide Bible Studies* (IVP).

Bible Concordances. A concordance will help you look up and study every reference that relates to the passage you are studying. They normally list every occurrence of a word in the Bible. A concordance can help you study a theme, such as prayer or love, through the Bible. Two popular concordances are *The Strong's Exhaustive Concordance* (Abingdon, Nelson, Riverside), and *The Young's Analytical Concordance* (Eerdmans, Nelson).

Bible Atlas. Geography played an important part in Biblical events. A good Bible atlas will show you places mentioned in the Bible. *The Pictorial Bible Atlas* (Zondervan) is a good one.

JUST REMEMBER IT.

Recently, I read about someone who purchased a Nolan Ryan rookie baseball card for only $12.00. The card normally sells for $1,200.00! Obviously, the clerk had made a mistake by not properly marking the card. When I read about the incident in *Sports Illustrated*—I had a sudden realization! I had collected that card in 1968 and had put it in a shoe box and tucked it away in a dark corner of my basement. I would never have realized the value of the card, unless someone had brought it's true value to my attention.

I'm convinced, that in a similar way, most people don't recognize the value of memorizing God's Word. Why memorize Scripture? There are several benefits to memorizing God's Word:

1. It will renew your mind. The first thing I learned about computers was, "Garbage in—garbage out." What you put into a computer determines what will come out. Your mind works the same way. What you spend time thinking about will show up in what you say and do. Scripture memory can reprogram your thinking, so that what you say and do will conform to God's standards. The goal of Scripture memory is to put God's Word in your mind, so that you can meditate on it and then obey it. The Apostle Paul explained how this process works, "And do not be conformed to this world, but be transformed by the renewing of your mind" (Romans 12:2).

2. ***It will keep you from sin.*** The psalmist said, "I have hidden your word in my heart that I might not sin against you" (Psalm 119:11). By internalizing God's Word he was able to be morally pure. When Jesus was tempted by Satan in the desert for forty days, he defended himself by quoting Scripture. It's been said that, "Sin will keep you from the Bible, or the Bible will keep you from sin." God's Word is either conforming you to His image, or you are being squeezed into the mold of the world.

3. ***It will help you better understand and apply God's Word.*** By meditating on Scripture you are able to think about how it applies to your life.

I've heard mediation compared to how cows "chew the cud." In the morning a milk cow eats grass for several hours like a lawn mower. Later in the morning, when it starts to heat up, they lay under a shade tree.

The cow begins to cough up little balls of grass they have swallowed earlier that morning. They will re-chew the cud, until they know they have gotten all the taste out of it. Finally, they swallow it into a second stomach compartment where it is digested and processed into the bloodstream. Chewing makes the digestion process easier. This makes for a healthy cow which produces wholesome milk.

Meditation on God's Word is a similar type of digestion. When you think on His Word, your mind will be filled with His thoughts and ways. Scripture memory helps you digest a scriptural truth by chewing on it over and over until you understand it and know how to apply it to your life.

When Should you Memorize?

Anytime! You can double your use of time by doing two things at once. You might memorize Scripture while you are exercising, or driving your car. Whatever works best for you, do it.

How to Memorize

1. *Review! Review! Review!* There are no secrets to memorizing Scripture. It takes time and effort. Repetition is the best way to remember a verse. After you've learned a verse, continue to review it.

2. *Include the reference and topic as part of the verse when you review it.* This will help you know what the verse means and where it is found. By doing this, you're more likely to remember the verse and where to find it in the Bible.

3. *Memorize Scripture with a friend.* This will give you encouragement and accountability. I've always found it was easier to work out with a partner in the gym, and this is true of memorizing Scripture.

4. *Apply the verse to your life.* The goal of Bible memory is not just head knowledge, but application. The Lord will help you in this process.

5. *Consistently memorize new verses each week.* After you have learned all the verses in the *Cross Training Workout*, begin to add your own. Add verses that impressed you from your Bible reading or verses that someone has shared with you.

6. *Copy the verse, topic and reference onto a small note card and carry this with you, as you review the verse.* You might stick the card on your bathroom mirror or some other place that would remind you to review the verse.

The *Cross Training Workout* provides you with a new Scripture every week. There are enough for one year, if you're memorizing one per week.

Get a grip on understanding and applying God's Word to your athletics and life. His Word provides the playbook for all we do. Even the most talented athlete falls short of their best performance without some plan or direction. No Christian, no matter how talented or gifted, can live the Christian life apart from God's Word. I suggest that you not only read this chapter several times, but also spend time thinking about how all this information applies to your life.

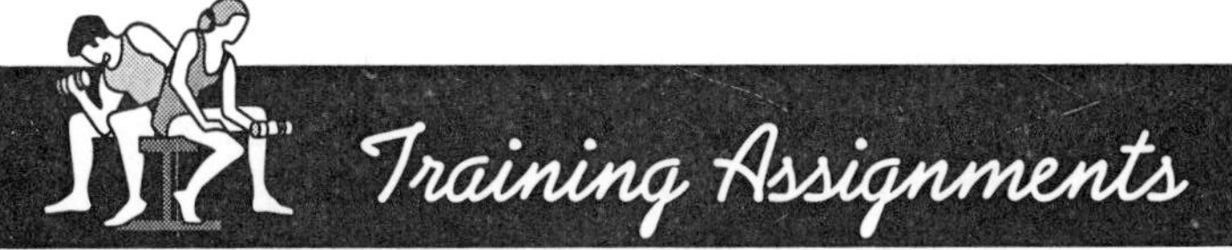

JUST REMEMBER IT.

"All Scripture is God-breathed and is useful for teaching, rebuking, correction and training in righteousness, so that the man of God may be thoroughly equipped for every good work" (2 Timothy 3:16).

JUST THINK IT.

I commit myself to regularly read, study, meditate on and memorize God's Word.

JUST DO IT.

Begin the Bible reading and Scripture memory program in the *Cross Training Workout*.

JUST PRAY IT.

"Lord, thank you for giving me your Word to guide me. Teach me how to grow spiritually through the study and application of your Word. Amen."

HUDDLE DISCUSSION

Cross Training Part 1

LEADING OFF: Who was your favorite coach when you were growing up? Why?

1. What is your favorite book of the Bible? Why?

2. What do you think? A = Agree D = Disagree

   a. The entire Bible is true.
   b. It's important to read the Bible.
   c. The Bible is a book of rules.
   d. The Bible doesn't apply to today's world.
   e. It doesn't matter what Bible translation you use.
   f. The Bible answers any of your problems.
   g. The New Testament is more important than the Old Testament.
   h. The Bible is written by God and men.
   i. The miracles in the Bible really happened.
   j. Science and the Bible are not compatible.
   k. The main theme of the Bible is salvation through Jesus.

3. How does the Holy Spirit help you understand the Bible?

4. Place an X on the line below nearest the number of minutes each day you think Christians should spend reading and studying the Bible. Explain your answer.

5. Which word best describes your Bible Study? Why?
Weak Fair Good Great Powerful

6. What are some of the benefits of reading the Bible?

7. Read each of the following scriptures and discuss it.

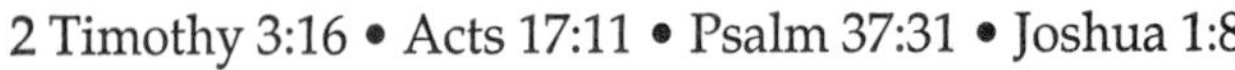

2 Timothy 3:16 • Acts 17:11 • Psalm 37:31 • Joshua 1:8

WIND SPRINTS

Cross Training Part 1

1. What is the role of the Holy Spirit? (See John 14:16).

2. Read Psalm 119. What does the Bible say about itself?

3. How can a friend help you grow spiritually? (See Proverbs 27:17).

4. According to Acts 17:11 what did the Bereans practice?

5. What does God's Word provide us according to Psalm 19:11?

6. According to the following verses what are some of the characteristics of God's Word? (See Joshua 23:14; Hebrews 4:12; Psalm 19:7-10).

7. What are some of the benefits of reading God's Word? (See Joshua 1:8; Psalm 37:31; Proverbs 6:22; Matthew 4:4; Psalm 19:8).

8. How does Scripture equip us for ministry? (See 2 Timothy 3:16, 17).

9. What should we do with God's Word? (See Luke 24:25; John 14:21; Acts 17:11; Colossians 3:16).

10. How can Scripture memory help you? (See Romans 12:2 and Psalm 119:11).

Spiritual Aerobics

"Prayer is the primary way that God transforms our lives. Prayer gives us spiritual power."

CHAPTER 8

CROSS TRAINING PART 2

At a recent national seminar for Christian teachers and workers, a survey was taken to determine the attitudes of the participants. One of the questions asked was, What will you be the most ashamed of when you get to heaven and what will you wish you would have changed? The overwhelming response was *My personal devotional life.*

Not only will many of us be ashamed of a poor devotional life, but we'll also miss the benefits that it brings to our spiritual life.

Those who watch sports don't receive the benefits of building strength, stamina, and speed. Only those who participate get the benefits—not the spectators. In your spiritual life you can chose to be a participant, rather than a spectator. If you're going to grow in your faith you need to get active. Get off the bench spiritually and get into the game. Just do it.

Every athlete knows the importance of balancing out their workouts with different exercises. In a similar way, God has given us several ways to exercise our spiritual muscles. The last chapter dealt with the spiritual disciplines for increasing your knowledge and application of God's Word. This chapter completes the *Cross Training Workout,* by covering how you communicate with God and others through prayer, witnessing, journaling, and note taking.

JUST PRAY IT.

What is Prayer? Prayer is the way we talk with God. Prayer is what helps us to carry on a relationship with Him. It's taking time to talk, listen and be in His presence. It includes telling God our thoughts and feelings. It involves confessing sin, worshiping God, giving thanks, and making requests for others and ourselves.

Real prayer is life changing. Prayer is the primary way that God transforms our lives. Prayer gives us spiritual power. John Wesley said, "God does nothing but in answer to prayer." There are many passages of Scripture that teach how God is able and willing to answer the prayers of his followers. The early church saw many answers to prayer. It has been said that when we work, *we* work; but when we pray, *God* works.

Eric Liddell, the Olympic champion runner who was the hero of the movie *Chariots of Fire,* understood the importance and power of prayer. His biographer quotes a woman who was in a prison with him during World War II:

> What was his secret? Once I asked him, but I really knew already, for my husband was in his dormitory and shared the secret with him. Every morning about 6 am, with curtains tightly drawn to keep in the shining of our peanut-oil lamp, lest the prowling sentries would think someone was trying to escape, he used to climb out of his top bunk, past the sleeping forms of his dormitory mates. Then, at the small Chinese table, the two men would sit close together with the light just enough to illuminate their Bibles and notebooks. Silently they read, prayed, and thought about what should be done. *Eric was a man of prayer not only at set times—though he did not like to miss a prayer*

meeting or communion service when such could be arranged. He talked to God all the time, naturally, as one can who enters the "School of Prayer" to learn this way of inner discipline. He seemed to have no weighty mental problems: his life was grounded in God, in faith, and in trust.[1]

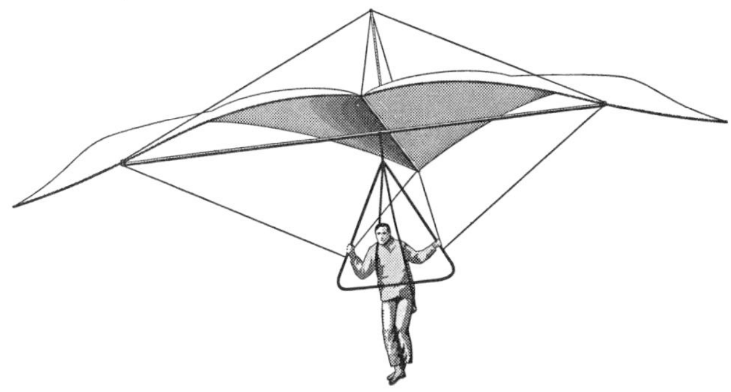

How to Pray

Being disciplined to pray each day is one of the most difficult, yet necessary, spiritual exercises in the *Cross Training Workout*. Jesus provides the model for how we are to pray. He said:

> "And when you pray, do not be like the hypocrites, for they love to pray standing in the synagogues and on the street corners to be seen by men. I tell you the truth they have received their reward in full. But when you pray, go into your room, close the door and pray to your Father, who is unseen. Then your Father, who sees what is done in secret, will reward you. And when you pray, do not keep on babbling like pagans, for they think they will be heard because of their many words. Do not be like them, for your Father knows what you need before you ask him."
>
> "This, then is how you should pray: 'Our Father in heaven, hallowed be your name, your kingdom

> come, your will be done on earth as it is in heaven. Give us today our daily bread. Forgive us our debts, as we also have forgiven our debtors. And lead us not into temptation, but deliver us from the evil one.' " (Matthew 6:5-13)

Based on this passage, Jesus' advice on praying is:

1. ***Pray secretly.*** Find a place that is away from distractions. Find a quiet place where you can pray without being interrupted. Jesus often prayed in a quiet place, "And in the morning, a great while before day, he rose and went out to a lonely place, and there he prayed" (Mark 1:35). This doesn't mean it's wrong to pray with others. In fact, it's become more common in sports to pray with teammates and even the opposing team following a game. It means that you should practice your personal prayer life away from distractions and interruptions.

2. ***Pray sincerely.*** Don't let your prayer life become meaningless. It's easy to let your prayer life become routine and boring.

3. ***Pray specifically.*** Don't just ask God to bless all the missionaries in the world. Be specific. A good way to be specific is to write down who and what you are praying for in the *Cross Training Workout* prayer journal.

PUMP HIM UP!
ACTS

One pattern for prayer is the ACTS acronym. The four letters stand for Adoration, Confession, Thanksgiving, and Supplication. These four elements should be present in a balanced prayer life.

Adoration

Prayer begins with God. "When you pray, say: 'Father' " (Luke 11:1-2). This Bible verse teaches the pattern of prayer. Jesus taught that you are to begin with God's concerns and interests first. It is a selfless kind of prayer because it is primarily for God.

If you don't start your prayer life with God, your prayers can easily become self-centered shopping lists. Adoration slows you down and helps you focus your attention on God.

Almost all adoration or praise fits into four categories:

1. The Name of God

In the Old Testament the name of Jehovah has several variations, all of them praiseworthy. For a complete listing of names check Nathan Stones, *Names of God*. Here are few examples:

- *Jehovah-Jireh:* provider (Genesis 22:14)
- *Jehovah-Shalom:* peace (Jud. 6:24)
- *Jehovah-rophe:* healer (Ex. 15:26)
- *Jehovah-rohi:* shepherd (Ps. 23:1)
- *Jehovah-m'kaddesh:* sanctifier (Lev. 20:8)

2. The Word of God

Two verses that focus on praising God for His Word are: "In God, whose word I praise, in God I have put my trust; I shall not be afraid" (Ps. 56:4).

"Then they believed His words; they sang His praise" (Ps. 106:12).

3. The Character or attributes of God

Most of us who follow athletics get excited about the performances of Michael Jordan or Bo Jackson. We call their dunks and touchdowns awesome! We praise their power and strength without any hesitation. But what about God? When the writer of Psalms describes God he says, "How awesome are your deeds! So great is your power that your enemies cringe before you" (Psalms 66:3).

You can praise God by meditating on His attributes. You might list the attributes or just focus on one. You could also read the Psalm in the reading plan or another that praises him. A few good ones are Psalms 8, 19, 23, 29, 30, 33, 46, 66, 100. Another way to adore God is to use the "ABC's of Praise". You start the ABC's of praise by going through the alphabet naming attributes or characteristics of God.

Here is a partial list of God's characteristics.

- Goodness (Ezra 3:11)
- Power (Ps. 21:13)
- Righteousness (Ps. 7:17)
- Everlasting loving kindness (2 Chron. 5:13)

Other attributes could include His holiness, grace, mercy, and many others.

4. The Works of God

Adoring God is simply praising Him for who He is and what He has done. Take a moment to tell God what you appreciate about Him. Here are a few of the things God has done.

- Healing (Luke 18:43)
- Help (Jer. 20:13)
- Works (Isa. 12:5)

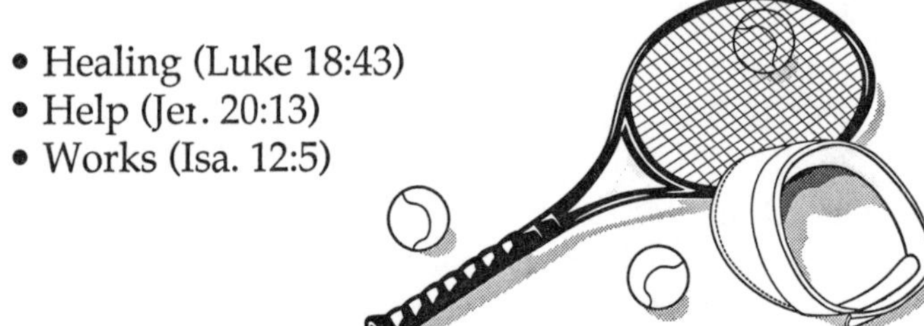

Confession

Confession is admitting your sin to God and then abandoning it. The Greek word for *confession* means "to say the same thing, to admit or declare oneself guilty of what one is accused of." When you confess your sin, you are agreeing with Him about the sin and seeing your sin from His perspective.

Confession should be sincere. In 1 John 1:9: "If we confess our sins, He is faithful and righteous to forgive us our sins and to cleanse us from all unrighteousness." Your confession should be specific acts, not sin in general. Scripture references: Psalm 51:17, James 4:6.

Thanksgiving

Thanksgiving is expressing your appreciation to God. Psalm 103:2 says, "Praise the Lord, O my soul, and forget not all his benefits."

Thank God for something specific He has done for you. You could thank God for spiritual, relational and material benefits and blessings. Take a moment each day to consider each category, and thank God for what He has done. Scripture references: 2 Corinthians 15:57, 1 Thessalonians 5:18.

Supplication

Once that you have adored him, confessed your sins and thanked him, you're ready to tell him about your needs. Supplication is asking for things, earnestly and humbly. It's asking for yourself and others. This is where you make your "petitions" to God.

God hears your prayers and answers them in three ways: yes, no, or wait. God knows what is best for you, so to those requests he says yes. He also knows what is bad for you, so he answers no. Some requests would be good for you sometime

in the future, so he says wait. Scripture references: John 16:24, James 5:16, Philippians 4:6.

What kind of Posture is Best?

There is not one posture or position that is best for everyone. Some like to get on their knees and pray, and some sit, stand, or walk. The important thing is that you are able to concentrate.

Suggestions for Making Requests

1. Pray according to God's will. (1 John 5:14-15). Don't pray for something that would violate the will of God. You will learn God's will when you study the Bible.

2. Don't make demands. Approach God humbly. Don't be arrogant when making your request. Your attitude should reflect that He is the boss, not you.

3. Persevere. It doesn't take much effort or faith to request something once. Often our time frame isn't the same as His.

4. Check your motives. Are you praying for reasons that will only serve you and not God? Ask yourself who will this request benefit? Why am I asking for this? It's always good to do a personal inventory of your motives. "When you ask, you do not receive, because you ask with wrong motives, that you may spend what you get on your pleasures" (James 4:3).

5. Pray believing in Jesus name. "And I will do whatever you ask in my name, so that the Son may bring glory to the Father" (John 14:13). This is not a magic formula, but the prayers of believers, doing God's work, will be answered. Our prayers are more than wishes, if we are believers, we can be confident that our prayers will be answered. Jesus said, "I tell you the truth, if you have faith, and do not doubt, ... you can say to this mountain, 'Go, throw yourself into the sea,' and it will be done" (Matthew 21:21-22).

Whatever your mountain is, the prayer of faith can remove it. It's important to keep in mind that faith comes from looking at God, not the mountain. In other words, don't focus on your problems or what you need, but rather focus instead on God and His ability to provide. Keep your attention on God's faithfulness, power and glory. If your prayers are consistent with the person and will of Jesus Christ, He'll hear and answer.

Timing

When should I pray? When you love someone you want to spend time with them. Prayer is the way we spend time with God. It's good to have a set time each day to pray for ourselves and others. I'm a morning person, but I know many others find the evening or noon hour to work best for them.

The Bible also says, "pray without ceasing" (1 Thess. 5:17). It is teaching us that we are not to restrict our prayer to a time period. The verse is telling us that prayer should be a way of life. There is nothing wrong with having a set time to pray, but it should just be a beginning.

What does it mean to pray without ceasing? It doesn't mean you have to walk around all the time with your eyes closed. What it means is that your heart should be open in constant communication with God. It's living with a constant awareness that God is with you. When you realize that God is always with you then you can constantly commune with Him.

The best way to illustrate praying without ceasing is to compare it to breathing. You can't just breathe every once in a while and live. You have to breathe all the time. It's easier to breathe than not to breathe. When you hold your breath you're fighting against the natural flow of breathing. The same is true of prayer. When you don't pray, you're holding your breath spiritually. Prayer should be a flow of life.

Using the Prayer Journal

Use the prayer journal in the *Cross Training Workout* to record your requests and God's answers. Writing down specific answers to prayer can reinforce your faith. A great motivator for prayer is answered prayer. Unless you take the time to record your requests, you'll never know how faithful God is in your daily life. I've found that when people use the prayer journal in the *Cross Training Workout*, they get excited to spend more time with God because they begin to see the results of their prayers. Your faith will grow as you see specific tangible answers to your prayers. Praying specifically is a great way to exercise your faith.

JUST SHARE IT.

What is Evangelism? The famous evangelist, Charles Wesley, was asked, "Why is it that people are so drawn to you—just like a magnet? People always seem to want to be with you. What is it about you that draws people?" Wesley's response was, "Well you see, when you set yourself on fire, people just love to come and watch you burn!"

That is what evangelism is about. The Greek word for evangelism means "good news" or "gospel." To evangelize is to spread the good news about Jesus Christ. If we know Jesus Christ, we will have a fire that burns within us. This fire draws others to us. Witnessing is a similar term used to indicate someone who testifies to who Jesus Christ is and what He does in people's lives.

Sharing our faith is a process of telling and living. People sometimes think it is only verbally telling someone about their faith. Others exclude telling others because they're uncomfortable, so they try to show them their faith by the way they live. Evangelism is both verbal and nonverbal communication. We must show them through our lives that Jesus is who the Bible says He is, and we must tell people what we believe. Both are necessary.

JUST LIVE IT.

Before we can tell people about our relationship with Christ, we must first earn the right to be heard. As Joe Aldrich, president of Multnomah School of the Bible says, "We must **be** Good News before we can **share** Good News." Jesus said, "Let your light shine before men in such a way that they may see your good works, and glorify your Father who is in heaven" (Matthew 5:16).

Tim Burke, pitcher for the New York Mets, when asked about sharing his faith said, "You think of soap boxes, preaching on the street about going to Hell. I don't preach to my teammates. Our walk is far more important than going up and preaching at somebody."[2]

In a sense, we are living Bibles read by others. The Apostle Paul had this in mind when he said, "You yourselves are our letter, written on our hearts, known and read by everybody. You show that you are a letter from Christ, the result of our ministry, written not with ink but with the Spirit of the living God, not on tablets of stone but on tablets of human hearts"

(2 Corinthians 2:3). Paul's point is that our non-Christian friends turn the pages of our life and examine the fine print. Many of our friends may not be willing to listen to an evangelist or some Bible teacher, but they will see us living our lives out. This is why it's so important that we not act one way and talk another. Always keep in mind that you may be the only Bible that someone will ever read.

JUST TELL IT.

The gospel includes the following:

1. The Old Testament prophecies about the coming King have been fulfilled by Jesus Christ. Jesus has come to save us "from the dominion of darkness" and to bring us into His kingdom (Colossions 1:13).

2. Everyone has violated God's standards. The Bible teaches us that we have all sinned and are separated from Him. The prophet Isaiah said, "But your iniquities [sins] have separated you from God...." (Isaiah 59:2). Sin is missing the mark of God's perfection, which results in spiritual death. Paul said in his letter to the Romans, "For all have sinned and fall short of the glory of God" (Romans 3:23).

3. God sent His son Jesus Christ to save us. Jesus was fully man, and fully God as the Son of God (Romans 1:3-4), so He was able to be the perfect sacrifice and bridge the gap between God and man. The Apostle Paul made this point when he said, "He died on the Cross and rose from the grave, He paid the penalty for our sins. "... Christ died for our sins ... he was buried ... he was raised on the third day according to the Scriptures and ... he appeared to Peter, and then to the Twelve. After that, he appeared to more than five hundred ..." (1 Corinthians 15:3-6). His resurrection is proof that He is God's Son.

4. Anyone who receives Jesus Christ into their life, will not die, but have eternal life. "But as many received Him, to them He gave the right to become children of God, even to those who believe in His name ..." (John 1:12). Faith is not just head knowledge or an emotional experience about Jesus Christ. The kind of faith in this verse describes a person who accepts something as true and relies on it as a way of life. James talked about a different kind of faith that was not saving faith. "You believe that there is one God. Good! Even the demons believe that—and shudder" (James 2:19). Saving faith is turning to God from sin. It's doing a spiritual U-turn. The Bible calls it repentance. Paul taught that , "Godly sorrow brings repentance that leads to salvation and leaves no regret...." 2 Corinthians 7:10).

To receive Christ you must:

- Admit you are a sinner and cannot save yourself.
- Repent and be willing to turn from your sin.
- Believe that Jesus Christ died for you on the cross.
- Receive, through prayer, Jesus Christ into your heart and life.

Many have found the "sinners" prayer to be a helpful way for people to confirm their commitment to receive Jesus into their life. The prayer isn't a magic formula. It's the attitude of your heart that God looks at. Most of these prayers go something like this:

"Lord Jesus, I need you. I know I am a sinner. I believe that you died for me on the cross and rose again. Right now I turn from my sin and put my faith in you as Lord and Savior. Thank you for saving me. Amen."

The Bible says, "...if you confess with your mouth, 'Jesus is Lord', and believe in your heart that God raised him from the dead, you will be saved ... for 'Everyone who calls on the name of the Lord will be saved" (Romans 10: 9,10,13).

Your Testimony

A personal testimony is simply you testifying to who Jesus Christ is and what he has done in your life. It helps others see how Christ came into your life, so that they don't see salvation as something mysterious or crazy.

Testimonies are similar, yet diverse. For example, I've heard people say, "I became a Christian at church camp when I was eight years old," or "I was involved with drugs when Jesus entered my life and changed me" or "I grew up in the church and always knew a lot about Jesus, but He didn't become real to me until high school." Just like each of these people, we're all saved in different ways and under different circumstances.

Your testimony is not any better or worse than any other. It's easy for Christians to fall into the trap of giving all of the attention to the radical conversions. A testimony that includes drugs, alcohol, and sex always gets more attention than the person who grew up in the church and has never done anything really bad. A radical conversion to Christ helps us see the power of God, but other kinds of testimonies are just as important, even if they seem boring to us. God uses many different kinds of testimonies to reach many different kinds of people.

Howard Johnson, the New York Mets' infielder who, like his former teammate Darryl Strawberry, became a Christian recently, commented on the difference between their testimonies, "I was the opposite of Darryl. He had such bad problems with alcohol and women. He hit bottom. I didn't. There are different ways to get the message."[3]

The early Christians were convinced of the importance of sharing their testimony. In the book of Acts it says, "Day after day ... they never stopped teaching and proclaiming the good news that Jesus is the Christ" (Acts 5:42).

Your Testimony Should Include:

- What my life was like before I received Christ.
- How I received Christ.
- What my life has been like since I received Him.

How To Share Your Testimony

- Make it sound conversational.
- Make the Bible the authority.
- Make it clear and brief.

Avoid:

- Using religious words and phrases. Phrases like "under the blood"
  and "prayed through" confuse the non-Christian.
- Glorifying the bad aspects of your life before Christ.
- Mentioning denominations or churches.

"How to" Resources on Sharing Your Faith

How to Give Away Your Faith, by Paul Little
Know What You Believe, by Paul Little

Know Why You Believe, by Paul Little
Becoming a Christian, by John Stott
Gentle Persuasion, by Joseph Aldrich
Evangelism Explosion, by James Kennedy
The Master Plan of Evangelism, by Robert Coleman

Materials to Share with Seekers

There are many books and tracts that you can give away to a friend who is seeking to know more about the Christian faith. Here are a few:

More Than A Carpenter, by Josh McDowell
Evidence That Demands A Verdict, by Josh McDowell
Steps to Peace with God, Billy Graham Assn. (Tract)
Step Up to Life, by Elmer Murdoch (Tract)
The Four Spiritual Laws, Campus Crusade (Tract)
More Than Winning, Fellowship of Christian Athletes (Tract)

Styles of Evangelism

Many people are scared of sharing their faith, because they think it means they'll have to embarrass themselves. Not everyone is called to be an evangelist, like Billy Graham. Bill Hybels, in his fine book, *Honest To God?*[4], mentions six possible styles of personal evangelism. They are: confrontational, intellectual, testimonial, relational, invitational, and serving. His point is that we don't all have to share our faith the same way. I think this is a good perspective of evangelism because it helps us realize we have a responsibility to share our faith, but we can do it in different ways. I'm sure there are as many styles of evangelism as there are people. Here is a brief explanation of each evangelistic style:

Confrontational Style

This type of person likes to hit you right between the eyes

with the gospel. They don't pull any punches. They're able to more naturally share their faith by confronting people face to face. A confrontational person likes to ask probing questions and challenge people to action.

The Apostle Peter was a good example of this style. He would often boldly preach and challenge people to respond to the gospel. He was always involved in the action and didn't mind creating a little controversy.

Intellectual Style

This type of person loves to debate. They enjoy logically examining the evidence for the gospel. The Apostle Paul is a good example of this style. He liked to use his education and intelligence to reason with people. He used this academic style at Thessalonica, "Some of the Jews were persuaded and joined Paul and Silas, as did a large number of God-fearing Greeks and not a few prominent women" (Acts 17:4).

Testimonial Style

This type of person simply tells what has happened in their life. These evangelists have not usually become Christians at an early age. Their stories of spiritual transformation are normally dramatic. An example of this style is the blind man in the book of John. "One thing I do know. I was blind but now I see!" (John 9:25).

Relational Style

A relational evangelist primarily shares their faith with those they're close to. In Mark 5 Jesus cast out a demon from a man who then wanted to join him. Jesus didn't let him come with Him. He said, "Go home to your family and tell them how much the Lord has done for you, and how he has had mercy on you" (Mark 5:19). This type of person dreads the thought of knocking on the doors of strangers to share their faith, but enjoys talking with those they already know.

Invitational Style

Some people might feel they can do very little to share their faith, since they don't fit any of the other styles. They may feel more comfortable as an invitational evangelist. This type of person invites friends to events that focus on pointing their friends to Christ. Most people come to know Christ because someone cared enough to reach out to them and invite them to church, concert, musical, retreat, movie, or some other event. After the Samaritan woman at the well (John 4) came to know Christ, she went back to town to ask others to come and hear Jesus for themselves.

Serving Style

Some people have the gift of serving others as a way of expressing the Gospel message. There are many people who know what to do to become a Christian. God may use the person who serves to soften their heart. An example of this style is Dorcas. In Acts 9 she impacted her city by doing deeds of kindness.

Did you relate to one style more than the others? Remember, you probably share traits of several. Regardless of your style, there will always be a time for you to tell it and live it.

The *Cross Training Workout* gives you a place to record the names of friends with whom you will share your faith in the future. This will remind you to look for ways to share your faith during the week, and remind you to pray for them.

JUST NOTE IT.

Why Take Notes? Hearing the Word of God taught by pastors and teachers can give you insights into God's Word. It can also help motivate you to live your life for God. The note-taking section of the *Cross Training Workout* is provided so that you can keep a record of what you've heard.

Sermons as well as Christian tapes are good resources for taking notes. You'll probably listen to 50-100 hours of teaching and preaching during the next year, so it's a good idea to try and retain some of it by taking notes.

JUST WRITE IT.

Why Journal? Recording the results of our time with God is one of the most important things we can do when we meet with Him. Keeping a journal is a way to listen to God and record what He is doing in your life. Many godly men and women have benefited from keeping a journal.

As a college football player, I was filmed during the practice sessions and reviewed the film the following day. As I watched myself on the big screen, I was able to learn from my successes and mistakes. When you journal you write down your successes and mistakes. By doing this, you can learn from your mistakes so that you make a better decision next time.

When you journal, you write down good moments as well as bad. Later you can go back and evaluate what God has been doing in your life. This helps to personalize your time spent with God.

Keeping a record of your time spent with God will help you better understand His values and His will for your life. There are times that I've learned insights into His Word by simply writing down the key thoughts from a passage of scripture.

While you can use the *Cross Training Workout* to record what God is saying to you from His Word, you can use the journal section for writing down your experiences, observations and reflections from the day.

How to Journal

Some people may write in this journal every day. Others may use it to write down how God worked in their life following a certain event or circumstance. Regardless of how often you do it, you'll benefit from seeing God's faithfulness in your life.

I have found a journal helpful for recording things that happened the preceding day. I'll jot down the people I talked with or the things I learned. You can use the space in the journal to write down impressions from God's Word, when you run out of space in your daily Bible reading section in the *Cross Training Workout*.

You'll see your faith grow as you feed it, nourish it, exercise it, stretch it, share it, and use it. When God's Word is read and applied, it's FANTASTIC!

JUST REMEMBER IT.

"Do not be anxious about anything, but in everything, by prayer and petition, with thanksgiving, present your requests to God. And the peace of God, which transcends all understanding, will guard your hearts and your minds in Christ Jesus" (Philippians 4:6,7).

JUST THINK IT.

I commit myself to pray and share my faith.

JUST DO IT.

Begin to use the prayer journal in the *Cross Training Workout* to record your prayer requests. Pray for someone to share your faith with.

JUST PRAY IT.

"Lord, Thank you for the opportunities to share my faith with others. Help me be bold enough to share how a relationship with Jesus Christ can change the lives of those I talk with. Amen."

HUDDLE DISCUSSION

Cross Training Part 2

LEADING OFF: What is your favorite sport? Why?

What will you be the most ashamed of when you get to heaven and what will you wish you would have changed?

Should an athlete pray openly before or during competition? Why or why not? Three examples of this are: 1) Orel Hershiser who gave an impromptu thanksgiving message on the mound after the 1988 World Series. 2) Prior to the 1986 Nebraska vs. Oklahoma football game, representatives from both teams met on the football field to pray before the game. 3) Following the Chicago Bulls 1991 playoff victory over the Lakers, the team recited the Lord's Prayer.

Rank the following spiritual disciplines from high priority (1) to lower priority (9): Discuss how and why you ranked them.

❍ Bible Study ❍ Memorizing Scripture ❍ Praying
❍ Fasting ❍ Worship ❍ Solitude ❍ Service
❍ Fellowship ❍ Confession

Which statement best describes your attitude toward witnessing? Why? Are you kidding? • Scared silly. • No problem sharing with close friends. • Can't keep my mouth shut.

It's more important to tell people about Christ then to live your faith out in front of them? Agree or disagree? Why?

Read each Scripture reference. After each statement, rate yourself from 1 to 5 on the scale by placing an X below the number that best describes you. Discuss each statement.

Most like Me 1———2———3———4———5 Least like Me

I spend time each day praying. (Mark 1:35)
I read the Bible daily. (Psalm 1:1-3)
I memorize at least one Scripture per week. (Psalm 119:11)
I seek guidance for my life from the Bible. (Psalm 119:9-16)
I share my faith at least once a week. (Acts 5:42)

WIND SPRINTS

Cross Training Part 2

1. Read Mark 1:35. Where do you hold your daily spiritual workouts?

2. How does Matthew 6:5-13 help us understand the pattern for prayer?

3. How should you pray? (See 1 John 5:14-15, James 4:3, and John 14:13).

4. What does it mean to pray without ceasing? (See 1 Thess. 5:17).

5. What kinds of things should you pray about? (See 2 Chronicles 7:14; Psalm 14:11; Psalm 143:10; Proverbs 3:5,6; Luke 22:31,32; James 1:5, James 5:16; 1 John 5:14).

6. As an athlete, how can you let your light shine? (See Matthew 5:16).

7. What kind of lifestyle should you maintain? (See 1 Timothy 1:7; 1 Peter 2:12).

8. Who's job is it to convert people? (See John 6:44).

9. What should you do before you share your faith with someone? (See 1 Thessalonians 1:5; 2 Corinthians 10:4,5).

10. Using the testimony outline in this chapter, prepare your own.

APPENDIX

Cross Training Publishing
P.O. Box 1541
Grand Island, NE 68802

JUST GROW FOR IT.

THINKING LIKE A BELIEVER

Philippians 3:13b-21

First Half

Devotion. The secret to progress in anything is to concentrate on "one thing." Too many Christians are involved in "too many things." As an athlete, you know the importance of devoting yourself to learning one play or technique at a time. As Christians, we need to devote ourselves to running the Christian race and letting nothing distract us. Read Phil. 3:13b.

1) What have been the results when you've concentrated on more than one sport or position at a time?
2) Is it better to excel at one sport or be average at several?
3) List the top five priorities in your life. Now share them with each other. Which ones do you most struggle to keep in perspective?
4) What does it mean to be devoted to one another?
(Romans 12:10).
5) About how much time do you devote to prayer and Bible study per week? (Joshua 1:8).
6) Are you satisfied with the amount of time you spend in Bible study and prayer? If not, arrange your schedule to include at least ten minutes more of each per week.

Second Half

Direction. An athlete seldom wins a race looking backward. Some Christians are distracted by past failures or successes and need to concentrate on the here and now. Read Phil. 3:13b.

7) What's worked best for you in shaking off an athletic loss and preparing for the next game?
8) What do you think it means "to forget" in Phil. 3:13b?
9) What happens to us when we dwell on our past mistakes? Our successes?
10) What does it mean to "set our minds on things above?" (Col. 3:2).
11) What are some of the things we should frequently focus on? (Phil. 4:8).

JUST GROW FOR IT.

COMPETING LIKE A BELIEVER

Philippians 3:13-16

First Half

Determination. "Aim at nothing and you'll hit it every time." The Christian has a clear-cut goal in his or her walk with God. If we're going to be effective in our service for God, we need to pursue God's goal for us with determination.
Read Phil. 3:14.

1) What are some personal goals you've set for yourself in athletics? Team goals?
2) How have they helped or hindered your performance?
3) What's the best prize or award you've ever received?
4) What do you think is "the goal" Paul mentions in Phil. 3:14 and how can it be reached?
5) What is "the prize" Paul talks about? How does it relate to your athletic competition?
6) If Christian athletes put as much determination into their spiritual lives as they do their sport, what difference do you think it would make?
7) Discuss the two extremes to avoid in Phil. 3:14: 1) "I must do it all" 2) "God must do it all"
8) What are some specific spiritual goals you can set this school year (prayer, Bible study, fellowship, & scripture memorization?

Second Half

Discipline. Without discipline an athlete probably won't win very often and will undoubtedly hurt his or her performance. No serious athlete can afford to compete without it. As Christians, the only way to obtain spiritual maturity and victory is through discipline. Read Phil 3:15-16.

9) Why is discipline so important to a team? What happens to a team when there is either too much, or too little discipline?
10) How does Phil. 3:16 relate to "the goal" God has given us? How would you define spiritual maturity?
keep pressing on toward spiritual maturity in this area?

JUST GROW FOR IT.

LIVING LIKE A BELIEVER

Philippians 3:17-21

First Half

Disciple. The term "disciple" is often used among Christians. We need to know what it means, what it involves and how it's to be carried out. Read Phil. 3:17.

1) Which coach or athlete has had the greatest influence on you athletically and why?
2) What is a disciple? Why would Paul ask others to follow his example?
3) Who is someone you know who has patterned their life after Jesus Christ?
4) What kind of an example have you been for others as an athlete? As a Christian?
5) How can we know for sure we're Christ's disciples? (John 15:5-14).
6) Read Matthew 10:38-39. What does it mean to "deny self"? "Take up your cross?" "Follow Christ?" "Lose your life?"
7) What's one change you'd like to make in your life that would make you a better disciple?

Second Half

Destiny. What about life and death? This is perhaps the most important question we can ask ourselves. The best answer is found in the Bible. Read Phil. 3:19-21.

8) If you were in charge of creating an amusement park ride called Hell, how would you make it real?
9) If the ride were called Heaven, how would you create it?
10) What would you have to do to get a ticket on each?
11) Share several ways to spend less time focusing on earthly things and more on eternal values.
12) If you knew you'd die in six months what, if anything, would you do differently?
13) How can you know for sure that you're going to heaven? (See 1 John 5:11-13).

NOTES

Chapter 1 - Winning: Win God's Way

1. "Tennis Was My Showcase," *Sports Illustrated*, August 28, 1989, p.76.

2. "That Was Then, This is Now," *Second Look*, July-August 1990, p.17

3. "Catching A Break," *Sharing the Victory*, April 1991, p. 4.

4. "Getting Down to Business,"*Sports Spectrum*, May/June, 1991, p. 9.

5. "Master at the Mid-Court," *Second Look*, Volume 1, Number 2, 1987, p.15

6. "Reaching The Top," *Sharing The Victory*, October 1990, p.6

7. "Playing The Percentages" *Second Look*, September-October, 1990, p.4

8. "The Gospel and Gaetti," *Sports Illustrated*, 1989, p.43.

9. "Pro Athletes Search for Fullfillment By Bringing Religion Into Their Lives," *New York Times* (April 29, 1991), p. C7.

10. "Pro Athletes Search for Fullfillment By Bringing Religion Into Their Lives," *New York Times* (April 29, 1991), p. C7.

11. "The Man in the Gray Hat." *Focus On The Family*, December 1990, p.21.

12. "Madison Square Gartner,"*Sports Spectrum*, November/December, 1990, p. 24.

13. "The King Refuses to Take the Throne," *Sharing the Victory*, May/June 1990, p. 5.

14. "Darryl Strawberry," *Sport*,, June 1991, p.32.

Chapter 2 - Goal: Pursue God's Goal

1. Gary Smalley, *The Key to Your Child's Heart* (Waco, Tex.: Word Books, 1984), pp. 109-110.

2. "The Defense Never Rests," *Second Look*, July-August, 1989, p. 6.

3. "Reaching The Top," *Sharing The Victory*, October 1990, p.6

4. Karen Drollinger, *Grace & Glory* (Waco, Tex.: Word Books, 1990), p. 57.

5. "The Two Heisman Man," *Sports Spectrum*, November/December, 1990, p. 28.

6. "Reaching The Top," *Sharing The Victory*, October 1990, p.6

7. Fritz Ridenour, *Life at Warp Speed* (Ventura, CA, Regal Books, 1990), pp. 132-133.

8. "Carrying A Big Stick," *Sports Illustrated*, May 8,1989, p. 5.

9. "They Did The Right Thing," *People Weekly*, Fall 1989, p. 127.

Chapter 3 - Motivation: Give All You've Got for God

1. Wilma Rudolph, *Wilma: The Story of Wilma Rudolph*, ed. Bud Greenspan (New York: New American Library, Inc., 1977).

2. "Bawl Players" *Sports Illustrated*, March 18, 1991, p.17.

3. Max Lucado, *The Applause of Heaven* (Waco, Tex.: Word Books, 1990), pp. 152-153.

4. "Master at the Mid-Court," *Second Look*, Volume 1, Number 2, 1987, p.16

5. "Athletes Who are Leading by Example," *Sports Spectrum*, March/April, 1991, p. 12.

6. "Quest for a Perfect 10," *Sharing The Victory*, May 1991, p.9

7. Karen Drollinger, *Grace & Glory* (Waco, Tex.: Word Books, 1990), p. 177.

Chapter 4 - Setbacks: Turn Setbacks Into Comebacks

1. "Vive LeMond!" *Sports Illustrated*, July 31, 1989, p.14.

2. "Clint Hurdles The Pressures of Hype," *Sports Spectrum*, November•December, 1990, p. 26.

3. "Rebounding In Rip City," *Sports Spectrum*, March/April, 1991, p. 8.

4. "Dan Reeves," *Sharing The Victory*, December 1990, p. 9.

5. "The Man in the Gray Hat." *Focus On The Family*, December 1990, p.21.

6. "Orel's Surgery." *Sports Spectrum*, January/February 1990, p. 5.

7. "The Most Outrageous Excuses of The Decade," *The National Sports Review*, 1989, p. 89.

8. "When The Comebacks Don't Come," *Second Look*, January-February, 1990, p. 6.

9. "Rebounding From Disappointment," *Athletes in Action*, Volume 1, Number
2, 1987, p. 9.

10. "Steeler Giant Refused to Quit," *Sharing The Victory*, September 1990, p.5

11. Tan, *Illustrations*, p. 1649.

12. "I Couldn't Doubt His Love," *Athletes in Action*, Spring, 1983, p. 44.

13. Karen Drollinger, *Grace & Glory* (Waco, Tex.. Word Books, 1990), p. 178.

14. "The Man in the Gray Hat." *Focus On The Family*, December 1990, p.21

15. "The Donnie Moore Tragedy," *The National Sports Review*, 1989, p. 20.

16. "Playing The Percentages," *Second Look*, September-October, 1990, p.5

17. "By the Grace of God...," *Sharing The Victory*, November 1990, p.16

18. "Knuckling Down to Business," *Second Look*, Volume 1, Number 1, 1987, p. 6.

19. "Knuckling Down to Business," *Second Look*, Volume 1, Number 1, 1987, p. 7.

20. Author unknown.

21. "A Hero At Home," *Focus On The Family*, January 1989, 1987, p. 19.

Chapter 5 - Ethics: Do the Right Thing

1. "An American Disgrace," *Sports Illustrated*, Feb. 27, 1989, p.16.

2. "Scorecard," *Sports Illustrated*, March 6, 1989 p. 12.

3. "Would You Buy a Used Sports Illustrated from this Man?" *The Christian Athlete*, 21, no. 4, 1977, p.18.

4. "NU's Osborne Not Concerned About Getting Raise," *The Grand Island Independent* (August 6, 1990), p. 1.

5. Karen Drollinger, *Grace & Glory* (Waco, Tex.: Word Books, 1990), p. 37.

6. "The Going Got Tough," *New Focus on Issues*", Volume 1, Number 1, 1986, p. 7.

7 "The Smut Stops Here," *Second Look*, Volume 2, Number 2, 1988, p. 14.

8. Bill Horlacher & Joe Smalley, *Grand Slam* (Here's Life Publishers: San Bernadino, CA, 1989) p. 16.

9. "Catching On In San Francisco," *Sports Spectrum*, November/December, 1990, p. 9.

10. "Barry Sanders: All-America," *Bigger, Faster, Stronger*, December 1988, p.3.

11 "I'm Sick and I'm Scared," *Sports Illustrated*, July 8, 1991, p. 21.

12. "Rebounding In Rip City," *Sports Spectrum*, March/April, 1991, p. 9.

13. Warren Wiersbe, *Meet Your Conscience* (Lincoln, NE: Back To The Bible, 1983), p. 6.

Chapter 6 - Teamwork: Teamwork that Works

1. "To Forgive, and Forgive," Guideposts, November 1990, p. 5.

2. "This Team Blended Together as One," *USA Today* (December 28, 1989), p. 1E.

3. "Dickerson Dilemma," *Sports Illustrated*, Oct. 22, 1990, p. 76

4. John R. Noe, *People Power* (Nashville, TN: Nelson Publishing, 1986), pp. 22,23.

5. "Inside Baseball," *Sports Illustrated*, May 13, 1991, p. 78

6. "Credit Another," *Sharing The Victory*, May 1991, p. 24.

Chapter 8 - Cross Training Part 2: Spiritual Aerobics

1. Sally Magnusson, *The Flying Scotsman* (New York: Quartet Books, 1981), p.165

2. "Pro Athletes Search for Fullfillment By Bringing Religion Into Their Lives," *New York Times* (April 29, 1991), p. C7.

3. "Pro Athletes Search for Fullfillment By Bringing Religion Into Their Lives," *New York Times* (April 29, 1991), p. C7

4. Bill Hybels, *Honest To God?* (Zondervan Publishing House, 1990), p.125.